Flying Feats

From the earliest balloon ascents in 1783 to Concorde and supersonic travel, the story of flight is one of adventure and excitement. Don Storer introduces some of the inventors, record-breakers and pioneers of the past two hundred years as well as aircraft such as the DC-3, the Wellington bomber, the fighter plane and the hang glider. You can take a trip to New York 1919-style or to South Africa 1932-style, fly around the Eiffel Tower in an airship or step into space with a Russian cosmonaut as you read these accounts of outstanding flying feats.

J. D. Storer is Assistant Keeper in the Department of Technology at the Royal Scottish Museum. He is the author of several books about flying and aircraft and runs an aircraft museum on the East Fortune airfield near Edinburgh.

FLYING FEATS

J. D. Storer

Illustrated by Peter Dennis

Beaver Books

First published in 1977 by
The Hamlyn Publishing Group Limited
London · New York · Sydney · Toronto
Astronaut House, Feltham, Middlesex, England

© Copyright Text J. D. Storer 1977
© Copyright Illustrations
The Hamlyn Publishing Group Limited 1977
ISBN 0 600 33613 1

Printed in England by Cox & Wyman Limited
London, Reading and Fakenham
Set in Monotype Baskerville

Contents

1   By balloon across the Channel 1785   7

2   By jet across the Atlantic 1974   11

3   Percy Pilcher's hang gliders of 1895   15

4   First step to the Moon 1961   20

5   Around the Eiffel Tower by airship
    1901   25

6   Around the world in 'easy' stages 1924   30

7   Igor Sikorsky and his flying machines   36

8   The end of the Schneider Trophy   42

9   One hour in the air   47

10   To New York and back in 1919   51

11   The battered Wellingtons   56

12 The wooden Mosquito 60

13 Amy Johnson's flight to Australia 65

14 By airline to South Africa – 1932 style 70

15 The first jet engine? 75

16 Faster than sound 80

17 From scouts to fighters 85

18 Malta's Gladiators 90

19 Forty years in service – the DC-3 story 95

20 Admiral Byrd's Polar flights 100

21 Flight over Everest 105

22 Walking in Space 110

23 The Berlin Air Lift 1948–9 115

24 One thousand miles an hour 120

25 Supersonic passengers – the Concorde story 124

1 By balloon across the Channel 1785

Dr John Jeffries was an American doctor living in London and his great interest was science, especially meteorology. The year was 1783, just a few years before the French Revolution began, but a year in which another kind of revolution took place in France. For the first time men were carried into the sky by balloons. Not surprisingly, Dr Jeffries followed these exciting events with interest. First the brothers Joseph and Étienne Montgolfier built a large balloon and filled it with hot air. Hot air rises and so the balloon floated upwards carrying with it two brave 'aeronauts', Pilâtre de Rozier and the Marquis d'Arlandes. Later in the same year balloons filled with the light gas hydrogen were invented by another Frenchman called Professor Charles. Balloon flights became a popular attraction and people paid to see these daring 'ascents'.

Balloons were not a very convenient way to travel, however, because they were at the mercy of the wind and could only go from A to B if the wind happened to be blowing in that direction. Several inventors tried to build balloons which could be controlled in flight with huge paddles but they had no success. One of these was yet another Frenchman, Jean-Pierre Blanchard, who brought his balloon to London in 1784 hoping to make a fortune with demonstration ascents. He met Dr Jeffries and took him for a flight – for a fee, of

course. They ascended from Mayfair, watched by the Prince
of Wales, and landed two hours later in Kent. Dr Jeffries took
with him some of his scientific apparatus, including flasks
which he intended to fill with rarefied air while they were high
above the earth.

Soon after this flight Blanchard and Jeffries started planning a more daring voyage – the first crossing of the English
Channel by air. Dr Jeffries was to finance the venture at a
cost of some £700, but this did not guarantee him a place in
the balloon. Blanchard was rather selfish and a bit of
a 'show-off', so it not surprising that he wanted all the
glory attached to this epic flight for himself. But Dr Jeffries
was equally determined that he too would make the crossing.

The great day approached at the end of 1784 and Blanchard's balloon was moved to Dover Castle. Once inside,
Blanchard locked the gates and refused to let his partner
through, but Dr Jeffries collected together some sailors and
they besieged the Castle. Fortunately the Governor of the
Castle was able to arrange a truce and the partners continued
their preparations for the flight. One of the tests they carried
out consisted of weighing all the items to be carried just to
ensure that the balloon could lift the full load – two men plus
all their equipment. Now, if this load proved to be too great,
something or someone would have to be left behind. Dr
Jeffries was surprised to find that his partner had put on a
considerable amount of weight since their last ascent. This
worried the Doctor, because he could see that the balloon
might be over-loaded and he knew who would be left behind.
On further investigation he discovered that Blanchard was
wearing a belt loaded with lead weights under his clothes!
Despite Blanchard's unsporting tactics the two men remained
partners and Dr Jeffries retained his place in the 'car' of the
balloon.

Blanchard's balloon was filled with hydrogen and, like
most balloons, it had one effective means of control – by
letting the hydrogen out through a valve the balloon would

sink back to earth. Most balloons started out carrying ballast such as sandbags which could be thrown overboard to lighten the balloon when the balloonist wished to gain height. Unfortunately, ballast cut down the useful load which might otherwise be carried. In addition to this up-and-down control, Blanchard fitted his balloon with wing-like paddles, a rudder and a primitive propeller to control his direction of flight. These were powered by the muscles of the two aeronauts and proved to be of no use.

On 7th January, 1785, everything was ready and the wind was blowing towards France. At 1 o'clock the heavily laden balloon lifted from the white cliffs of Dover and drifted slowly out to sea. All went well, but in order to maintain height the two men had to throw ballast overboard at frequent intervals, and by the time they were two-thirds of the way across the Channel all the ballast had gone. The balloon was still sinking towards the sea. The two aeronauts had to lighten the load still further, so overboard went their brandy, the wings and propeller, anchors and ropes and various other items, but still the balloon descended. Blanchard even threw away his coat, Jeffries followed his example, and then Blanchard's trousers went overboard! The sea was drawing very close so they put on their cork life-jackets and braced themselves for the splash. Then quite suddenly the balloon started to rise, and at 3 o'clock they crossed the French coast.

They landed almost naked in a quiet forest some twenty kilometres from the coast but later in the day they received a tumultuous welcome in Calais, where their 'car' is still preserved in the Museum. Blanchard was given a prize and a pension by King Louis XVI of France, but Jeffries received nothing more than the honour of becoming the first fare-paying international air traveller in the world – the first of many millions.

2 By jet across the Atlantic 1974

On Sunday 1st September, 1974, a sleek black jet aircraft touched down on the runway at Farnborough in Hampshire where it was to appear in the International Air Show. It had flown from its base in the United States, and although there was nothing too unusual about that, it had earned a place in the record books. This Lockheed SR-71A 'Blackbird' had just broken the New York-to-London record by crossing the Atlantic in under two hours – 1 hour 55 minutes and 42 seconds, to be precise. It had covered 5633 kilometres in approximately the same time it took Blanchard and Jeffries to cross the English Channel by balloon in 1785!

Blanchard and Jeffries would have found it very hard to imagine an aircraft cruising at 1817 miles an hour (2924 kph), compared with their modest ten miles an hour (16 kph). Even today this speed is breathtaking – we can imagine a car travelling at a speed of 30 mph (48 kph), but the SR-71A averaged 50 kilometres per minute. After landing at Farnborough the pilot, Major James Sullivan, explained that it took 320 kilometres to slow down before he could approach the runway. His landing speed was an amazing 170 mph (274 kph), and this is faster than many light aircraft can fly. Major Sullivan and his crew member, Major Noel Widdifield, received an enthusiastic welcome from their wives, officials and reporters.

This was the happy ending to a story which had begun many years earlier in great secrecy.

In 1960 the United States Air Force wanted a supersonic fighter capable of flying at three times the speed of sound (Mach 3). It also had to be capable of operating at a height of 80,000 feet (24,400 metres). Naturally these plans were kept very secret, but there were problems. The most powerful high-speed aircraft become hot due to friction caused by their metal skin moving through the air. Most metals grow weaker when they are heated, and the aluminium-based metals used to build aeroplanes were no exception. At speeds of over twice the speed of sound (Mach 2) these aluminium alloys were just not strong enough, so the American designers decided to use the heavier metal titanium. The new fighter YF-12A made its first flight in April 1962 and 93 per cent of its metal parts were made from titanium. Only three planes were built, but nevertheless the YF-12A made the news in 1965 when one aircraft broke two world records with a speed of 2070 mph (about 3330 kph) and a flight at an altitude of 80,258 feet (24,463 metres).

The military experts changed their minds and decided that, instead of a Mach 3 fighter, what they really needed was a 'spy-in-the-sky' aircraft. A long-range strategic reconnaissance version was ordered, and this was called the SR-71A. Because of its ability to fly fast and high the SR-71A would be able to fly over foreign countries without being intercepted. The first one flew in December 1964, and just over a year later the first Blackbird entered service with the United States Air Force at their huge Beale Air Force Base in California. The Blackbird is painted black all over, but its shape is not very bird-like. It is a very long aircraft with a triangular or 'delta' wing on which two large and powerful engines are fitted. The thrust from these engines can produce a maximum speed of 2300 mph (3700 kph), and yet the Blackbird carries enough fuel for a flight of 3500 miles (5600 kilometres). For longer flights it can be refuelled in the air from tanker aircraft. The

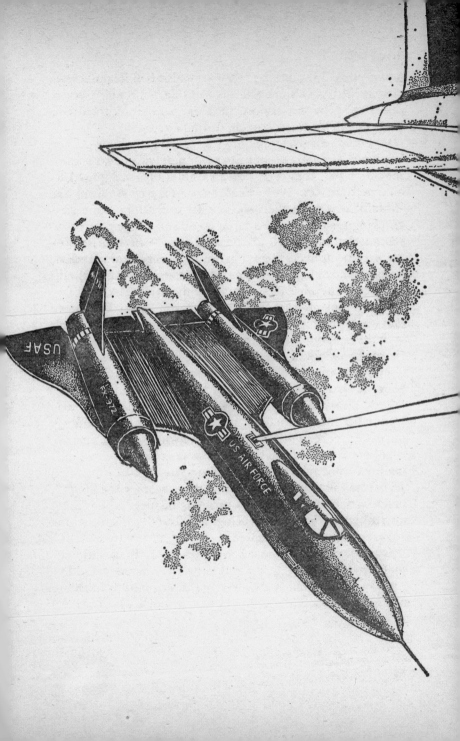

amazing performance of this reconnaissance aircraft never caught the public's imagination until Farnborough International 1974, by which time the design was ten years old – a long time in the fast-changing world of aviation.

Although the New York-to-London flight took less than two hours, the crew were on board for nearly six hours because they took off from their base in California some 4000 kilometres from New York. Even before take-off Sullivan and Widdifield were in their cockpits for a considerable period, checking all the complex equipment and plugging in their special clothing. Their astronaut-like suits had to be pressurised to protect them against the very low pressures encountered at high altitudes and water-cooled to combat the heat from the aircraft's skin when flying at Mach 3. Two SR-71As took off from the long runway at Beale. The second one was a reserve aircraft just in case there was any trouble with the first, but it was not needed and returned to base. The record-breaking SR-71A was refuelled twice in the air from Boeing KC-135Q tankers before it crossed the starting line or 'gate' at New York. The London 'gate' was about 5600 kilometres away, but as the aircraft's range was also 5600 kilometres, there was always the chance that it might just run out of fuel, particularly if there were any headwinds. This risk could not be taken, and the SR-71A was refuelled again during the record run from a tanker aircraft off Newfoundland. Of course the refuelling cost some time, because the SR-71A had to reduce height and slow down to the speed of the tanker aircraft while the fuel was being transferred. This makes the record even more remarkable.

On the return flight another crew flew the Blackbird back to its base and set up a new record between London and Los Angeles. Today this flight by a non-stop scheduled airliner takes eleven hours – the Blackbird flew home in 3 hours 47 minutes.

3 Percy Pilcher's hang gliders of 1895

Hang gliding has become a very popular sport in recent years, and anyone who has seen these graceful flying machines in action must have been impressed by them. These impressions may range from sheer panic at the thought of jumping off a cliff supported only by a flimsy triangular wing to a feeling of elation at being able to fly like a soaring bird.

The desire to fly like a bird has been one of man's ambitions for centuries, but for a very long time the bird-men made the mistake of trying to copy sparrows instead of seagulls. A sparrow flies by flapping its wings vigorously, whereas a seagull has a lazy flapping action and for long periods does no flapping at all – it just soars through the air. The early bird-men usually jumped off towers, flapped their wings and crashed to the ground. They did not have sufficient strength in their muscles for wing-flapping flight. Then in the 1880s a German engineer called Otto Lilienthal made a study of birds, especially soaring birds, and at last the day when a man could fly with wings drew nearer.

Otto Lilienthal built his first glider in 1891 and tried to launch himself into the air from a springboard, but this did not work. Perhaps Lilienthal should have taken into account the fact that birds do not use a springboard but they do make use of the wind blowing up a slope. Lilienthal very sensibly copied the birds and started gliding down a gentle slope. He even built an artificial hill, fifteen metres high, near Berlin and made about two thousand flights before he was killed in a gliding accident in 1896. His work was carried on by a British engineer called Percy Pilcher.

Percy Sinclair Pilcher was born on 16th January, 1867 in Bath, and at the age of thirteen joined the Royal Navy as a cadet. When he left the Navy he served an apprenticeship in marine engineering with Randolph, Elder and Co. in Glasgow, and went on to study engineering at London University. In 1892 Percy Pilcher returned to Scotland as assistant to the Professor of Naval Architecture and Marine Engineering at Glasgow University. Percy's sister Ella moved to Glasgow with him and they made many friends, for they were described as 'bright, clever and attractive' and Ella was an accomplished singer. Despite Percy's professional interest in the sea his hobby was in the air, and he read the reports of Lilienthal's experiments with growing interest. He started to make flying models but his landlady objected and the Pilchers had to find new lodgings.

Pilcher decided to build a full-size glider early in 1895. He had seen pictures of Lilienthal's machines but decided to start from scratch with his own design. He called this first glider the 'Bat', and very wisely decided to visit Lilienthal before venturing into the air. In April he went to Germany and watched Lilienthal successfully flying his hang glider. Lilienthal hung by his arms in the framework of the glider, leaving his legs free to run downhill for take-off and to balance the glider in flight. For example, if he wished to make the glider dive he would swing his legs forward – this would make the machine nose-heavy, and put it into a dive. Learning to balance a glider was not easy and Pilcher obtained some useful hints from Lilienthal. One lesson Pilcher did not take to heart concerned the need for a tailplane (or horizontal rudder); he discovered this in June when he tried to fly his Bat, which did not have one. In his own words Pilcher said: 'Lilienthal told me that a horizontal rudder was absolutely necessary. I would not believe him, but found out that he was quite correct.' So the Bat was modified and Pilcher made his first short flights.

Percy Pilcher had other problems to contend with. He lived in Glasgow, so he had to build his glider in the city and then transport it into the country to make a flight. To do this he made the wings collapsible, rather like two huge fans held in shape by many wires. The wings were covered with a light sail fabric as used by racing yachts, and expertly sewn together by his sister Ella. She also acted as workshop assistant, general porter and first-aid attendant. Pilcher's early flights were made at Wallacetown Farm, Cardross, on the north bank of the River Clyde some thirty kilometres from the centre of Glasgow. It was an ideal site with a gentle slope facing into the prevailing winds blowing across the wide Clyde valley, and there were few obstructions or spectators.

After several flights in the Bat, Pilcher built his second glider, the 'Beetle', which was larger and much heavier. In fact it weighed 80 lb (36 kilos) compared with 45 lb (20 kilos) for the Bat, and of course Pilcher had to run along carrying this weight until he became airborne. He soon abandoned the Beetle and rebuilt the Bat.

Early in 1896 Percy Pilcher built another large glider which he called the 'Gull'. On calm days he needed a large glider to lift him into the air, although a small one was enough for a breezy day. Unfortunately calm days did not always remain calm, and several times the Gull was damaged by the wind. It was abandoned.

About this time Pilcher moved south to Eynsford in Kent, where he worked for the famous inventor Sir Hiram S. Maxim. Maxim had already invented a machine-gun and a huge steam-powered aeroplane which almost flew. Here Pilcher built his fourth and most successful glider, the 'Hawk'. Again it was a small hang glider with folding wings made from light-weight bamboo members covered with fabric and braced with wires. One new addition was an undercarriage with sprung wheels to make landing more comfortable. This was

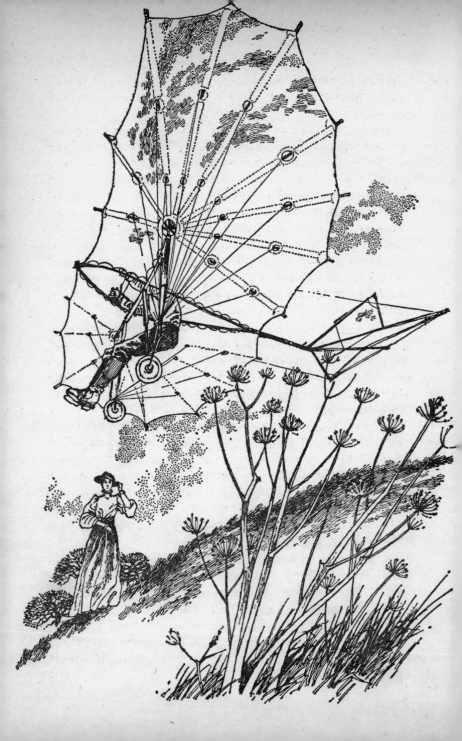

the first sprung undercarriage in history, and almost all aeroplanes today have sprung undercarriages as a matter of course.

In June 1896 Pilcher again visited Lilienthal and found that he was experimenting with biplane gliders. These were very similar to the original monoplanes but had a second wing added above the pilot's head. Pilcher was invited to fly one of these and, although impressed, decided they would not stand up to the gusty winds he encountered at home. During the summer of 1896 the Hawk made a number of good flights, but the site in Kent was not very suitable for slope soaring and Pilcher introduced a new method of launching. He was towed into the air using a towline – rather like a kite – with his hardworking assistants pulling on the line. Again this was an innovation which became widely used.

Pilcher was eager to build a powered aeroplane, and in 1896 he designed one based on the Hawk and powered by a small petrol engine. He patented the design but could not find a suitable engine, so in 1898 he left his job and set up a company to develop an engine in partnership with Walter G. Wilson. Although this work took up most of his time, Pilcher still flew the Hawk occasionally and increased his record to a distance of 750 feet (230 metres). He also designed a glider with four wings but never flew it.

During August 1899 Pilcher's new engine was tested, and on 30th September he crashed while demonstrating the Hawk glider at Stanford Hall in Leicestershire and he died two days later. Would he have beaten the Wright brothers and become the first man to fly in a powered aeroplane? No one can tell, of course, but he was well on the way. His famous Hawk hang glider was repaired and is now on display at the Royal Scottish Museum in Edinburgh.

4 First step to the Moon 1961

'. . . five, four, three, two, one . . .' – a deep roar and a long slender rocket lifts off its launching pad at Cape Canaveral in the United States. The date is 5th May, 1961 and inside the tiny Mercury spacecraft is Astronaut Alan B. Shepard Jr on his way up to a height of 115 miles (185 kilometres). A few days later on 25th May, President John F. Kennedy announces that an American will set foot on the moon by 1970. So began man's first step to the moon – less than seventy years after Lilienthal and Pilcher made their first short flights into the air.

The very first man in space was the Russian 'cosmonaut' Major Yuri Gagarin, who made an orbit of the Earth on 12th April, 1961 – just a few weeks before Alan Shepard's straight up-and-down flight. Both these spacemen were carried into space by rockets which were related to the simple firework rocket. The great advantage of a rocket is that it can operate without any air, and of course in space there is no air. A jet engine would be useless because it needs the oxygen in air to make its aviation fuel burn. A rocket burns fuel too, but it carries its own supply of oxygen: some rockets carry liquid oxygen while others make use of chemicals rich in oxygen, such as hydrogen peroxide (also used to bleach hair).

Of course the rocket had come a long way from the simple

firework to the man-carrying space vehicle, and many inventors had helped it on its way. Perhaps the most famous
name in rocket history was Dr Wernher von Braun, the German
scientist who helped to develop the V-2 rocket missile during
the latter years of World War Two. The V-2 was fired from
sites in northern Europe and aimed at targets in the south of
England. It carried almost 1000 kilos of high explosive and
could reach targets 320 kilometres away from its launching
pad. Because it travelled at 3600 mph (5800 kph) it could not
be intercepted by fighter aircraft and so it was a formidable
weapon. When the war ended most of the German rocket
experts were encouraged to continue their work either in
Russia or the United States. Von Braun continued his work
in America where he became even more famous.

Both the Russians and the Americans started by building
rocket missiles developed from the V-2 and later turned their
attention to peaceful space research. In 1958 the Americans
founded their National Aeronautics and Space Administra-
tion, or NASA as it is more usually called, to organise their
activities in space 'for the benefit of all mankind'. Just six
months later newsmen were invited to NASA headquarters
for a special announcement: 'Gentlemen, these are the
astronaut volunteers'. Behind the speaker sat seven smart
young men. They were to take part in 'Project Mercury',
which aimed to put a man into space as soon as possible –
preferably before the Russians. The seven Mercury astronauts were very carefully selected from over four hundred
volunteers. They were all military test pilots of the very
highest standard, and all less than six feet tall (1.83 m) as
the Mercury spacecraft was too small for anyone taller.

Alan B. Shepard Jr was born on 18th November, 1923,
and was 35 years old when he was selected as an astronaut.
During the war Shepard served in the US Navy as an officer
on a destroyer and only started flying after the war, in 1946.
He served with a Navy fighter squadron and later became a
Navy test pilot. By 1958 he had spent over three thousand

hours in the air, and when Project Mercury was announced he was desperately keen to try his hand in space.

For two years the Mercury astronauts were given a most strenuous training course consisting of advanced academic studies mixed with physical exercises and tests which resembled medieval torture. Many lectures had to be attended on subjects ranging from astronomy to the theory of gyroscopes, and then the astronauts had to learn how to fly a spacecraft. When learning to fly an aeroplane a student pilot is taken up in a plane with dual-controls but this was not possible in space, so the student astronauts had to learn how to fly their spacecraft while still on the ground. They learned to fly in a series of imitation spacecraft called 'simulators', which could do almost anything except fly. Making sure that the astronauts could stand up to the stresses and strains of space flight involved some very strenuous tests, such as being spun round in a huge roundabout or 'centrifuge' which subjected each man to a force of ten times his normal weight.

Alan Shepard passed all his tests and was chosen for the first Mercury launching in his spacecraft *Freedom 7*. All the Mercury spacecraft had names ending with '7', because there were seven astronauts involved in the programme. *Freedom 7* was mounted on the nose of a 'Redstone' rocket originally developed by von Braun and his team as a medium-range missile. The Redstone was not powerful enough to put the Mercury spacecraft into an earth orbit, and the more powerful Atlas rocket was needed to do this. The first two Mercury flights were therefore planned as up and down flights to test the spacecraft and the method of recovery when it splashed down into the sea.

In the early hours of 5th May, 1961 Alan Shepard got dressed for his big day. This took him some time because not only did he have to put on a complicated space suit, but he also had to be 'wired up' to several instruments. These would measure his heartbeat, temperature and breathing rate during the flight and transmit their information by radio to the

ground controllers. By 6.10 in the morning Alan Shepard was strapped on his couch in *Freedom 7* and the door sealed. He was ready to go but then there was a problem. Some unexpected clouds had appeared in the sky and these would interfere with the view of the flight by the ground observers, so the start was delayed. Poor Alan Shepard had to wait for over three hours in *Freedom 7* until the weather conditions improved, then at 9.34 a.m. the Redstone lifted off. After two minutes its work was done and the Mercury spacecraft separated from the rocket and continued on its way into space. For about five minutes Alan Shepard was weightless in space, then he had to face the problem of re-entering the Earth's atmosphere.

The Mercury spacecraft was bell-shaped and it flew into the air blunt end first because this section was made of a special material to withstand the heat generated by the terrific air resistance. This 'heat shield' actually got so hot that it burned, but it was thick enough not to burn away completely. Alan Shepard guided *Freedom 7* back safely and it parachuted down in the sea some 500 kilometres from his launching site after a flight of fifteen minutes. His 'hop' of 115 miles (185 kilometres) up into space prepared the way for space flight just as Lilienthal and Pilcher's hops in their gliders prepared the way for aeroplane flight. Alan Shepard was luckier than the glider pioneers, for he survived to see how things developed and even took part in a later space flight in 1971, when he landed on the Moon.

5 Around the Eiffel Tower by airship 1901

Alberto Santos-Dumont was the son of a wealthy Brazilian coffee planter and became famous in France for his adventures in the air. In fact, during 1906 many people in Paris thought that he was the first man to fly an aeroplane.

On 23rd October Santos-Dumont made a short flight in a strange box-kite aeroplane of his own design which flew tail-first. Few people in Paris had heard about the Wright brothers' flights in America, as these had been deliberately kept secret by the Wrights because they were afraid of people stealing their ideas. So the flight by Santos-Dumont was thought to be the world's first. The aviator himself made no such claim as he was well aware of the Wrights' achievements, but his was the first officially-observed flight in Europe and this was only one incident in an action-packed life.

Alberto was brought up on his father's plantation in Brazil, where his interests included reading the futuristic stories of Jules Verne and driving his father's locomotives. At the age of fifteen he saw a balloon ascent in São Paolo and begged for a flight, but his father refused to let him go because of the danger to life and limb. At eighteen Alberto was sent to Paris to continue his studies, and while in Paris he met some French balloonists who took him up for a flight. Alberto was very impressed, and afterwards wrote: '. . . it seems not to be the balloon that moves, but the earth that sinks down and away.' He was determined to continue flying and made a number of adventurous balloon ascents before turning his attention to the design of airships, or dirigible (steerable) balloons as they were sometimes called.

Alberto Santos-Dumont built his first airship in 1898. It was little more than a sausage-shaped balloon fitted with the small petrol engine from his own De Dion motor-tricycle. By 18th September 'Number One' was ready for its first flight from the Zoological Gardens in Paris. Santos-Dumont took off down wind – following the advice of his balloonist friends – and crashed into the treetops. Two days later he tried again, this time taking off into the wind, and all went well for a while as Number One climbed up into the sky to a height of about 450 metres. But in order to descend Santos-Dumont had to release some of the gas, and with less gas inside it, the sausage-shaped balloon began to lose its shape. Eventually it folded in the middle and started to fall towards a field where some boys were flying kites. Santos-Dumont shouted down to the boys to catch the end of a long rope hanging down below the airship and to run into the wind. Luckily they understood and Number One returned to earth more like a giant kite than an airship. The shaken Alberto resolved to fly at lower altitudes in the future.

A year later the young Brazilian built his Dirigible No. 2 but this crashed into some trees and was wrecked. No. 3 followed shortly afterwards in November 1899, then came No. 4, and with each design Santos-Dumont became more and more experienced. He built a shed in the grounds of the Paris Aero Club at Saint Cloud and his exploits began to capture the imagination of the public. In 1900 a wealthy oil magnate called Henri Deutsch de la Meurthe offered a huge prize of 125,000 francs for the first person to fly from Saint Cloud, round the Eiffel Tower and back to Saint Cloud in under thirty minutes. The distance was only about eleven kilometres but it was a formidable challenge in 1900 and one Alberto Santos-Dumont could not resist.

Dirigible No. 5 was ready for an attempt early in the morning of 13th July, 1901. With a following wind, Santos-Dumont reached the Eiffel Tower in good time but when he headed back towards Saint Cloud with the wind now against him he made little progress. Then his engine failed and he landed in yet another tree. He was lucky to escape once again and even luckier when the Brazilian Princess Isabel who was living nearby sent along a picnic basket with a fine breakfast in it. She later gave him a charm to protect him against all accidents – whether he needed it or not is a good question, for few aviators survived more mishaps than the dashing Alberto. Dirigible No. 5 was repaired for a second attempt on the prize a few weeks later. Once again the dirigible rounded the Eiffel Tower, met a headwind and then had engine failure. This time the gas in the sausage-shaped balloon exploded and observers thought the intrepid aviator had been killed. But the Princess's charm must have worked because he landed unhurt on the roof of a six-storey hotel.

Meanwhile Dirigible No. 6 was being built and this was prepared for a third attempt on 19th October, 1901. Once again the wind was rather strong, but in the early afternoon Santos-Dumont took off and within nine minutes he reached the Eiffel Tower. He rounded the tower watched by many spectators and headed for home against the wind. For the third time his engine stopped but on this occasion he climbed along the open framework of his airship to the engine and managed to restart it. This delay left him very little time to get back to Saint Cloud within the time limit of 30 minutes. In fact he reached the landing ground in 29 minutes 31 seconds but did not have time to actually land his airship. The official judges said he had failed, but Henri Deutsch accepted that he had arrived in time and handed over the 125,000 francs. Santos-Dumont gave some of the money to his mechanics and the rest to charities. This flight created a sensation in Paris, and at last the public began to take a real interest in flying.

Santos-Dumont did not stop here: he went on to build

eight more airships and his every escapade was followed with interest. He became the first airship pilot to land in the sea when he 'ditched' in Monaco Bay during 1902. Dirigible No. 8 was flown by Mademoiselle d'Acosta – the first woman to fly an airship. But the tiny Dirigible No. 9 became his most popular 'mount', for he used it rather like a horse to travel around the wide streets of Paris. As one account says, 'He actually proceeded along the streets of Paris to his house early one morning and alighted at the door, leaving the balloon in the roadway whilst he entered and partook of breakfast, then entering the car (i.e. the airship's car) again ascended and made his way to the starting place.' On other occasions he landed at his favourite cafés and tied the airship to a convenient lamp-post while having a drink!

The last of Santos-Dumont's dirigibles was No. 14, for by 1906 his interest had switched to aeroplanes. His first aeroplane was called 14-bis because he tested it slung underneath Dirigible No. 14 before taking off on the first flight in Europe. The most famous Santos-Dumont aeroplane was his tiny Demoiselle (i.e. Dragonfly), with a wing span of only 18 feet (about 5.5 metres). It proved to be very popular with sporting pilots and could claim to be the forerunner of many light aeroplanes suitable for private owners. Few men played such an active part in early aviation as the popular Alberto Santos-Dumont: the famous cross-Channel pilot Louis Blériot said of him, 'You are our Pathfinder'.

6 Around the world in 'easy' stages 1924

In 1901 the Brazilian airship pioneer Santos-Dumont won a prize of 125,000 francs for flying round the Eiffel Tower, and only twenty years later men were planning to fly around the world. By 1921 the Atlantic had been conquered and flights to Australia and South Africa had been achieved, so the next step was to tackle a world flight. There were many hopeful contenders including teams from Britain, France, Italy, Spain, Argentina, Portugal and the United States. A large and efficient team was essential because this was no daredevil dash – such a flight required careful organisation to ensure that supplies were ready and waiting at all the planned stops. There were very few aerodromes available in the 1920s and most of the stopping places were in the middle of nowhere.

In 1923 the United States Army Air Service decided to attempt a round-the-world flight, and they set about it in a big way. Most teams prepared one aircraft for the flight, but the Army Air Service decided to use four so that at least one of them would stand a good chance of completing the journey. Other teams sometimes used old and unsuitable aircraft, but the American aircraft were specially designed for the project by a leading designer called Donald Douglas, who later became world-famous for his airliners. To back up their project the army were promised help by the United States Navy, Diplomatic Corps, Bureau of Fisheries, Coast Guard

Service and even American companies with overseas branches. But perhaps most important in the planning of such a flight was the selection of crews. Each aircraft carried a pilot plus an engineer, and when the news of the flight was released hundreds of men volunteered. Four pilots and two reserves were selected. Each pilot was allowed to choose his own engineer – it was important that they had complete confidence in each other for an adventure such as this.

One of the pilots, Lieutenant Erik Nelson, spent many days at the Douglas factory in Santa Monica, California, supervising the building of the 'World Cruisers'. Donald Douglas with his theoretical ideas, and Erik Nelson who was a tough practical flier, did not always agree and they had many long arguments, but between them they produced a world-beater. The new aircraft were biplanes with a wing-span of 50 feet (about 15 metres) and were powered by a single 450-horsepower Liberty engine. They could be fitted with wheels for land use or floats which would enable them to operate from any convenient stretch of water. Great attention was paid to the problems of servicing under difficult conditions, such as changing an engine without a crane. Although tools, spares and equipment were to be sent to the planned stopping points, each aircraft had to carry a considerable load of equipment in case it was forced down between bases. Consequently only a limited amount of fuel could be carried and this reduced the World Cruiser's range to approximately 1300 kilometres. Flights of 650–950 kilometres were planned, which on paper looked like easy stages, but fate and the weather could make even a short flight hazardous. Because of these relatively short hops many refuelling stops were going to be needed in order to cover the total distance of about 40,000 kilometres. In fact twenty-two foreign governments were asked for permission to land in or fly over their territory.

By April 1924 everything was ready – the four aircraft were fitted with their floats and were based on Lake Washington near Seattle in the north-west of the United States. The start

31

was fixed for the 4th but it was too foggy. Next morning Major Frederick L. Martin and Sgt Alva Harvey in the flagship *Seattle* opened up their engine for take-off, but the propeller broke and so the start was again delayed. Finally on 6th April the great flight began but not without another incident. Lieutenant Leigh Wade and Sgt Henry Ogden could not get their aircraft *Boston* to lift off the water, so they stopped and threw away an anchor, a rifle, their spare boots and sundry other items. This did the trick and they were able to make a belated start, but then they had to fly the first stage alone through fog, rain and snow. Flying low to avoid the fog, they almost hit two ships. When the fliers arrived at Prince Rupert, having covered 1050 kilometres in just over eight hours, the Mayor of this Canadian town greeted them with: 'Gentlemen, you have arrived on the worst day in ten years!' Flying around the world was not going to be easy.

The American plan was to fly up the west coast of Canada, then across the North Pacific to Japan, India, Europe, Greenland and back to the United States. By choosing this route the fliers would have to face some of the worst conditions in early stages, but they were extremely fit and well prepared. However, conditions were even worse than they expected, with fog, snow, ice and strong winds, so they could not relax for a minute in the air. Even on the ground they had problems – one afternoon Erik Nelson was walking to the post office when he noticed that one of the World Cruisers had broken loose from its anchor and was drifting towards some rocks. He had no choice but to wade into the icy sea to hold it off. When they flew north to Alaska conditions grew even worse, and Major Martin in *Seattle* ran into trouble. First he had to make a forced landing on the sea when his engine failed, but a new engine was brought by a Coast Guard cutter and fitted into the aircraft by lantern light in a snowstorm. With the new engine Major Martin managed to take off despite the rough sea and set out to rejoin the others. After a stop to refuel he took off again on a hop which involved flying over mountainous

country. Fog enveloped the *Seattle* and it hit a mountain. Luckily both crew members escaped the crash and survived the long trek to civilisation, but for them the world flight was over. The other three aircraft continued their journey and arrived in Japan two months after they had left Seattle. In these two months they had flown on only ten days – such were the difficulties of flying in Alaska and neighbouring territories.

From Japan things went more smoothly, yet there were still adventures. Lt Lowell H. Smith had taken over the leadership in *Chicago* since Major Martin's crash, but he too nearly came to grief in Indo-China. Smith and Lt Leslie Arnold had engine trouble and landed on a remote lake in the jungle. They managed to persuade the local natives to man three war sampans and tow *Chicago* some forty kilometres along the river to the nearest town, where a new engine duly arrived and was fitted in record time. The three aircraft continued through Burma to India, where they discovered a stowaway. When Lt Leigh Wade and Henry Ogden landed at Allahabad they were surprised to see American reporter Linton Wells climbing out of their tool compartment. The extra weight had not been noticed because the World Cruiser's heavy floats had been replaced by lighter wheels as they were now flying over land. Using surface travel, Wells had found it difficult to keep up with the fliers now that they were progressing more quickly, so he decided to join them! He was allowed to fly on to Karachi before the order came to leave him behind.

From India the three aircraft continued across the Middle East and Europe to Britain, where their crews received an enthusiastic welcome at Croydon Airport before flying on to Brough near Hull. Here at the Blackburn Aeroplane Company's works the World Cruisers were converted back to seaplanes ready for the North Atlantic crossing which was to start from Scapa Flow in the Orkney Islands. Everything had been going well across Europe, but soon after the fliers' departure from Scapa Flow they ran into their old enemy – fog. *Chicago* and *Boston* turned back, but Nelson and Harding in *New Orleans*, having lost contact with the others, flew on and reached Iceland despite nearly crashing into the sea. A few days later *Chicago* and *Boston* took off from Scapa Flow and headed for Iceland, but *Boston* had engine trouble and had to land on the sea. Wade and Ogden were rescued, but while their aircraft was being towed to safety it capsized and sank. The other two aircraft continued to Greenland and Canada, where a replacement aircraft, *Boston II*, was waiting so that Wade and Ogden could rejoin the flight for the final stages across the United States. Everywhere they landed the fliers were mobbed by enthusiastic crowds. The flight ended on 28th September, 1924 after covering 26,345 miles (42,398 kilometres) in about seventy 'easy' stages.

7 Igor Sikorsky and his flying machines

A few people become world-famous during their lifetime, but Igor Ivan Sikorsky was unusual – he did it three times! He was born on 25th May, 1889, in the Russian city of Kiev, where his father was a professor and his mother a doctor. It was very rare for a woman to be highly educated in Russia at that time, but Igor's mother was no ordinary woman. She did not read her son stories from the usual children's books, but instead told him about aviation and, in particular, the ideas and experiments of Leonardo da Vinci.

Leonardo lived about 400 years earlier. He was a great Italian painter and dreamt up some wonderful inventions, including flying machines. Young Igor was fascinated by Leonardo's idea of a helicopter, and at the age of twelve he built a model of one, powered by rubber bands, which actually flew.

Igor was educated at the Naval Academy in St Petersburg, and then went on to study engineering at the Polytechnic Institute in Kiev. During his time at school the Wright brothers made their historic first flight by aeroplane and Igor followed their progress with great interest. His determination to study aviation grew, but there was virtually no aviation to study in Russia so when he left college in 1908 he decided to go to Paris. His sister Olga, who was a teacher, encouraged him and even gave him money to buy an aero engine. In Paris the

nineteen-year-old Igor met many of aviation's pioneers and discovered that they were not at all keen on the idea of a helicopter – they had plenty of problems with the relatively simple fixed-wing aeroplane. Igor returned to Kiev still convinced that he could design a helicopter and in 1909 he put his ideas to the test using the Anzani engine he had bought in Paris. The first Sikorsky helicopter did not fly, nor did the second. Young Igor realised that his friends in Paris were right and he turned his attention to fixed-wing aeroplanes.

In 1910 the first Sikorsky biplane was built and ready for its test flight, but the S-1 would not leave the ground. A more powerful engine was fitted into the S-2 and Sikorsky was able to make a few short hops. These experiments were costing a fair amount of money which the Sikorsky family could ill afford, but they had faith in Igor's ability and with their continued support he went on with improved designs. By the summer of 1911 he built the S-5 which remained in the air for an hour, and the following year he was made Designer and Chief Engineer of the aircraft division of the Russia-Baltic Wagon Factory (RBVZ).

Sikorsky designed several small aircraft and then turned his attention to a revolutionary large aircraft. This was to have a huge wing span of 92 feet (28 metres), four engines and an enclosed cabin for passengers and pilot. All these features were considered impossible by many experts in 1912. Its sheer size was frightening, for it was twice as big as other large aeroplanes and the first aircraft in the world to be fitted with four engines. Sikorsky was also told that a pilot must sit with at least his head in the airstream in order to judge the aircraft's manoeuvres, but he was an experienced pilot himself and insisted on an enclosed cockpit.

The new machine was officially named Russian Knight, but because of its size it was generally called Le Grand. On 13th May, 1913, it was ready for its first flight with Igor Sikorsky at the controls – he was eager to test his theories and, not being superstitious about the date, took off. The giant biplane lifted into the air and after a short flight Sikorsky was mobbed by an enthusiastic crowd. Le Grand made fifty-three flights before it was badly damaged on the ground by an engine falling from another aircraft!

Sikorsky's next design was even larger. It was a four-engined bomber called Ilya Mourometz after a Russian hero. The first flight took place in January 1914 and a month later it established a world record by carrying sixteen passengers and a dog to a height of 6560 feet (2000 metres) over Moscow during a five-hour flight. About eighty similar aircraft were eventually built and they were widely used by the Imperial Russian Air Service during the First World War. Sikorsky was rich and famous, but then the Russian Revolution broke out and he decided to emigrate to the United States.

When Igor Sikorsky arrived in New York in 1919 he was almost penniless and could only speak a little English. There was no work for aircraft designers because the war had just ended and there were many surplus aircraft available at bargain prices. For several years Sikorsky almost starved. Eventually he founded a new company with the help of a few Russian friends who had also emigrated to America. They started to build a twin-engined airliner, the S-29-A (A for America), under extremely difficult conditions. Because the company was so short of money, the workers had to build the aircraft in the open and often without pay. Parts were obtained from a number of unlikely places including junk yards and cheap chain stores. At one time the project was in more serious financial trouble than usual, and all seemed lost, when the famous Russian composer Rachmaninoff came to the rescue with a donation of $5,000.

By 4th May, 1924, the S-29-A was ready for the first flight. All the workers wanted to be on board and poor Igor did not have the heart to refuse them, so the overloaded aircraft took off – and crashed. Luckily there were no serious injuries but the aircraft had to be rebuilt. Next time all went well and the S-29-A was a success. Incidentally, it finished its career disguised as a Gotha bomber which crashed in the early flying film *Hell's Angels*.

The Sikorsky Aero Engineering Corporation grew from these simple beginnings into a large and successful company. Igor Sikorsky made his name in Russia with large land-planes, but in America he is remembered for his great flying boats of the 1930s. The S-38 amphibian, which could operate from land or water, was built in 1928 and used by several American airlines for pioneering new routes. The first four-engined S-40 flying boat was christened *American Clipper* by Mrs Hoover, the President's wife, in 1931 and many Clippers were to follow. Perhaps most famous was the very advanced S-42 of 1934 which soon established ten world records for load-carrying. Pan American Airways used the S-42 on their new routes to Bermuda and South America. They were also making experimental flights across the Pacific and Atlantic when the Second World War intervened.

Meanwhile the Sikorsky company had been taken over by the United Aircraft Corporation and merged with another company to become Vought-Sikorsky. Igor was once again a world famous figure in aviation, so when he asked for permission to return to his first love, the helicopter, his directors could hardly refuse. In the corner of a factory in Stratford, Connecticut, Igor Sikorsky started another career. By autumn 1939 a helicopter, designated the VS-300, was ready for testing, and of course the chief designer insisted on flying it himself – a most unusual arrangement in the aviation business. Igor strapped himself into the seat of his weird tubular contraption which had a large rotor above his head and a small sideways-facing propeller at the tail. He was wearing his ordinary hat and coat – in fact he did not intend to go very far because the new helicopter was tethered to the ground just in case it was difficult to control. Of course there was a long way to go before helicopters went into service, but, as the general manager said, 'Before Igor Sikorsky flew the VS-300 there was no helicopter industry; after he flew it, there was.'

Sikorsky helicopters led the world. They were the only helicopters used by the United States during the Second World War. For the third time Igor Sikorsky had become famous, yet he was still a quiet, modest man when he retired in 1957. When he died in 1972 aviation lost one of its greatest all-rounders.

8 The end of the Schneider Trophy

Jacques Schneider came from a wealthy French family and his hobbies included aeroplanes, balloons, speed boats and racing cars. Unfortunately a serious accident on the Monte Carlo motor-racing circuit left him with an injury which restricted his participation in hobbies, so he turned his attention to organising sporting events.

Schneider noticed that most of the aviation competitions were for land planes and decided to encourage seaplane racing. In 1912 he presented an impressive trophy made of gold, silver and bronze which was to be presented to the fastest water-based aircraft flying round a set course. Any country could enter a team of three aircraft and the winning country would be responsible for organising the next race. One further rule – any country winning three times in five years would keep the trophy permanently.

The first Schneider Trophy contest was held in 1913 at Monte Carlo in the Principality of Monaco. Each seaplane was to be timed over a course of twenty-eight laps around a ten-kilometre circuit, making a total distance of 280 kilometres. This proved to be too long for most of the competitors, and only one finished without long stops for repairs. The winner was a French pilot, Maurice Prévost, in his little Deperdussin monoplane racer converted to a floatplane, and his speed was only 45.75 mph (73.63 kph). Actually his speed would have been 61 mph (98.17 kph), but he taxied over the finishing line instead of flying over and the judges made him take off again and complete another lap!

Monaco was chosen for the second race in 1914, and this time there were competitors from five countries. The winner was a tiny British Sopwith Tabloid biplane flown by Howard Pixton and his speed was 86.78 mph (139.61 kph). This may not seem fast, but it was too fast for two of Pixton's rivals who were due to follow him, and they dropped out of the competition. The Tabloid was another land plane fitted with floats, so Schneider's aim to provide races for genuine seaplanes was not entirely successful. For the next four years the First World War prevented further races but the Tabloid, fitted with wheels, was in the news again when it served with the Royal Flying Corps in France as a scout aircraft.

In 1919 the contest was arranged at Bournemouth and the British entered a Supermarine Sea Lion. This was a genuine water-based aircraft – a flying boat. Unfortunately all the competitors got lost in a sudden blanket of fog and the race was abandoned. Italy won the next two races, then a Supermarine Sea Lion II won for Britain, and this was followed by a win for the United States in 1923. There were no opponents in 1924, but the Americans did not fly over the course and claim a 'walk-over' victory. Instead they went ahead with the 1925 arrangements for a contest at Baltimore.

An exciting race was forecast. The Americans had their very fast Curtiss biplanes, while the Italians pinned their hopes on two flying boats and the British entered with two Gloster biplanes and the revolutionary Supermarine S.4 monoplane designed by R. J. Mitchell. This was just the kind of contest Jacques Schneider had envisaged, with top class seaplanes competing for the most famous speed event in the world. Indeed several of the entrants during the 1920s and '30s were also holders of the outright world speed record. The Supermarine S.4 broke the world speed record for seaplanes before the 1925 race but crashed during trials and the

Americans won again. Because these racing seaplanes were so expensive, Britain was finding it difficult to compete every year and had requested that the Schneider Trophy should be held every two years.

When the 1926 contest was announced Britain did not enter but the Italians, encouraged by their new leader Mussolini, designed and built a new monoplane. This Macchi M.39, with a powerful Fiat engine, narrowly defeated the American biplanes and thus ended not only the biplane's domination but also American hopes of an outright victory. The Schneider Trophy would continue, but for how long?

Venice was the location chosen by the Italians for the 1927 race. The American Government had withdrawn its support but the British Government decided that the Royal Air Force should enter. Because the S.4 had been so promising, R. J. Mitchell of Supermarines was asked to design a new machine. Two Supermarine S.5 monoplanes were built and together with a Gloster biplane they made up the British team to face the three Macchi M.52s of Italy. These Italian seaplanes were powered by very highly-tuned engines which proved to be unreliable and they all dropped out – as did the Gloster biplane. So the two S.5s with Napier Lion engines came in first and second, flown by Flight Lieutenants S. N. Webster and O. E. Worsley. The winner's speed was 281.65 mph (about 453 kph).

The International authorities agreed to hold the event every two years from 1927 onwards, so Britain began preparing for the 1929 contest which was to be held at Calshot on Southampton Water. Once again it was only a two-nation event between an Italian team and an RAF team of two new Supermarine S.6s and one S.5. The S.6 was developed from the S.5 but was fitted with a Rolls-Royce R engine of 1900 horsepower which was twice as powerful as the Napier Lion. The Italians decided to run their engines at reduced power to improve their reliability, but two of their pilots had to retire when they were overcome by smoke and fumes. One of the

S.6 pilots could not see very well when he lost his goggles and turned inside one of the pylons marking the course – he was disqualified. Flying Officer H. R. Waghorn in the leading S.6 ran out of fuel on his last lap and thought he had lost, but he had miscounted and was actually flying an extra lap when his fuel ran out! His speed was 328.63 mph (about 529 kph), in second place was the only Italian survivor, and then came the S.5.

Now Britain was in a position to win the Schneider Trophy outright during the 1931 contest. Perhaps the most exciting part of this contest was the pre-race drama as Britain struggled to raise a team. The new Labour Government refused to give financial support and for a while all seemed lost, then Lady Houston came to the rescue with a gift of £100,000 towards Britain's entry. It was still quite a struggle to obtain permission for the RAF to compete, but in the end all was set for a great contest between the improved Supermarine S.6B and the exciting new Italian seaplane, the Macchi-Castoldi MC.72. Unfortunately the Italians could not get their aircraft ready in time and Flight Lieutenant J. N. Boothman flew an S.6B over the course at Calshot unopposed to win the Schneider Trophy outright for Britain. Jacques Schneider did not see the end of the Schneider Trophy, for he died in 1928.

The story does not quite end here, however, for the S.6B went on to increase the world air-speed record to 406.99 mph (655 kph), only to be beaten later by the MC.72 which achieved 440.68 mph (709.21 kph). The lessons learned in these contests were invaluable, and R. J. Mitchell used them all when he produced his next high-speed aircraft – the Supermarine Spitfire.

9 One hour in the air

No one is really sure who made the first aeroplane flight – if you count a short hop into the air as a 'flight'. But there is no doubt who made the first real flights in an aeroplane which could be controlled in the air – the American Wright brothers. For the first ten years in the history of the aeroplane Wilbur and Orville Wright were ahead of the rest of the world. Of course their first flight in 1903 is recorded in the history books, but some of their other remarkable achievements are less well known. For instance in September 1908 Orville remained in the air for one whole hour when his nearest rival in Europe had just achieved twenty minutes and in Britain no one had yet flown in an aeroplane.

Wilbur and Orville were the sons of a bishop and lived in Dayton, Ohio. As the boys grew up they developed an interest in mechanical things, but most of the time they had to teach themselves and consequently became very self-reliant. They started designing and building printing machines, then they switched to the bicycle business, and this remained their main source of income while they experimented with gliders and aeroplanes.

It was Wilbur who first really studied the art of flying, but Orville soon followed and they both read about the exploits of the early gliding pioneers such as Otto Lilienthal. The Wright brothers realised that the hang gliders used by these pioneers were not suitable for conversion into a powered aeroplane: the difficulty was one of control. The hang gliders were controlled by the pilot swinging his legs about to change the balance of the glider, and this just was not good enough for a heavier and faster machine. Wilbur had studied the flight of birds, particularly the graceful gliding buzzard, and realised that the flow of air had to be used to control the movements of an aeroplane. A rudder which steered like a ship's rudder, and an elevator to control climbing or diving had already been tried out by other people, but the Wright brothers devised a method of twisting the wings to make the aircraft bank or roll. This was their secret of success.

In 1900 Orville and Wilbur Wright started by building and flying gliders to test out their ideas on control. Having mastered the art of gliding they looked around for a suitable engine but they searched in vain. Eventually they set about designing an engine of their own and a propeller for it. By 1903 their first aeroplane or 'Flyer' was ready for testing. On 14th December all was ready, and the brothers tossed a coin to decide who should make the first flight. Wilbur won, but he tried to climb too steeply and the Flyer 'stalled' back to earth. There was no serious damage to man or machine, and by 17th December, 1903 they were ready again. This time it was Orville's turn. He took off and landed safely twelve seconds later, but on the fourth and last flight of the day Wilbur remained airborne for 59 seconds and covered 852 feet (about 260 metres). This was only a beginning.

A new Flyer was built in 1904 and made about eighty flights including some simple manoeuvres such as a circular flight round the field. The longest flight achieved by Flyer II was 5 minutes 4 seconds. During the following year Flyer III was built. This is sometimes described as 'the World's first practical aeroplane', because it was strong enough to fly regularly and could perform complicated manoeuvres such as figures of eight. The Wright brothers made several flights of half an hour's duration in Flyer III, and one of 38 minutes 3

seconds. Then for a period of two and a half years the brothers did no flying at all, and it was during this time that Alberto Santos-Dumont made the first flight in Europe – 21 seconds in the air. But the Wright brothers were not relaxing – far from it – they were busy building new aeroplanes.

In May 1908 the brothers were ready to fly again and a very exciting few months followed. They started by practising with the old Flyer III, which had been rebuilt and converted to carry a passenger. On 14th May Mr Charles Furnas, one of their helpers, became the first aeroplane passenger to make a real flight when he was taken on a trip of more than three kilometres. Some of these flights were seen by reporters, who were hiding near the field used by the Wrights. It seems rather strange, but all the Wright brothers' flights were made in secret – they were so afraid of someone stealing their ideas. Therefore, little was known in Europe of their achievements, but the European pioneers were about to have a surprise.

By the end of May 1908 Wilbur arrived in France with one of their new Model 'A' biplanes packed in crates. The work of assembling and preparing the new machine took rather a long time, and the French aviation experts became very critical. Then Wilbur announced that his first flight in the new machine would be made in public. Now this was also the first ever public demonstration by the Wrights, and naturally the European aviators and reporters were very curious. On 8th August Wilbur took off and astounded all the critics. They were amazed to see how beautifully the Wright biplane flew under complete control, making smooth banked turns in contrast to the rather erratic manoeuvres of the European aeroplanes. One famous French aviator exclaimed: 'Well, we are beaten! We just don't exist.'

Meanwhile, back in America, Orville was preparing another Model 'A' for trials by the US Army which were to be held at Fort Myer near Washingdon DC. The trials began on 3rd September, 1908, and for the first time in America a Wright aeroplane flew in public. Orville made ten flights during which he was airborne for a total time of nearly six hours, and on several occasions he carried a passenger. He established an altitude record of 200 feet (about 60 metres) and then broke it by reaching 310 feet (about 95 metres). But his most impressive flight was made on 9th September. In the morning he circled the army camp for 57 minutes, and in the afternoon remained airborne for 1 hour 2 minutes 15 seconds. No one could doubt that the aeroplane had 'arrived'.

10 To New York and back in 1919

When the First World War ended many airmen found it difficult to settle into routine jobs, so they set about conquering the continents and oceans of the world by air. One of the most challenging feats was a flight across the Atlantic Ocean. Back in 1913 the Daily Mail had offered £10,000 for the first crossing in less than 72 hours. A crossing was made in May 1919 by an American flying boat, but it made several stops and took two weeks. The prize was won by Captain John Alcock and Lieutenant Arthur Whitten-Brown, who made a non-stop flight from Newfoundland to Ireland in June 1919 using a converted Vickers Vimy bomber. Another historic Atlantic flight was made by Charles Lindbergh in 1927, when he flew solo non-stop from New York to Paris. The first non-stop flight in the opposite direction has never received the publicity it deserved, yet it took place just a couple of weeks after Alcock and Brown's crossing and long before Lindbergh's flight.

The story starts with an incident during the war. A German airship L33 – one of the dreaded Zeppelins – was shot down over England in September 1916. The L33 was damaged by fire but her main shell was intact, so the British experts were able to examine her in detail. Now this was a lucky break, because German airships were far superior to British ones at the time. In November 1916 the British Government decided to build three airships based on the design of the L33. One of these was ordered from William Beardmore and Company of Glasgow and given the number R34. Work started in December 1917 at Inchinnan on the south bank of the River Clyde, but the war ended before R34 was completed. However work continued, and in May 1919, after two test flights, she was ready for the short flight across Scotland to her 'station' at East Fortune, 32 kilometres east of Edinburgh. Unfortunately she ran into fog and then darkness fell, and R34 remained in the air twenty-one hours before she was able to land!

The Government decided that His Majesty's Airship R34 (or *Tiny* as she was called by her crew) should fly to New York and back as an exercise. Incidentally her crew of thirty were RAF officers and men, although they usually wore Royal Navy uniforms and the officers held Army ranks. The airship's Captain was Major G. H. Scott, but also on board was Britain's senior airship officer Brigadier-General E. M. Maitland. To add to the confusion *Tiny* was anything but tiny – she was longer than two football pitches end to end, or 643 feet (about 196 metres) to be precise, and she had five engines.

Soon after midnight on Wednesday 2nd July, 1919, the giant airship was brought out of her hangar and last-minute preparations made. Then, as Brig.-Gen. Maitland wrote in his log: '1.42 a.m. At a signal from Scott, the bugle sounds the "Let go", the huge Airship slowly rises . . .' On their way out towards the Atlantic the crew could just make out the Forth Bridge, then later the R34's birth-place at Inchinnan, and Loch Lomond. The R34 cruised at 50–55 mph (80–90 kilometres per hour), so the 5000-kilometre flight to New York was going to take several days. The crew was divided into two 'watches', which took it in turns to man the airship. In fact in many ways it was more like sailing a ship than flying an aircraft – for instance the crew slept in hammocks and the steering was done by a coxswain. Even the routine chores had their lighter side – one crew member became the first person to peel potatoes while flying the Atlantic! To keep the crew entertained during their off-duty time, the R34 carried a gramophone and the latest jazz records.

After lunch on the first day an unusual discovery was made, when one of the crew found a stowaway on board. The stowaway was no stranger, because he was one of the original crew members who had been left out at the last minute in order to reduce the airship's load. Young William Ballantyne was determined to go on the flight, so he had hidden on board just before take-off. The officers were sympathetic but he was reprimanded and put to work in the galley or pumping petrol. Later in the day another stowaway was discovered – a tabby kitten.

On Thursday one of the engines gave trouble when its water jacket started to leak. It was repaired with a piece of copper sheeting and the crew's entire supply of chewing gum – hastily chewed by the Engineer Officer and two of his men! By Friday afternoon the R34 was flying over Newfoundland where some letters were dropped by parachute. But there were still about 1450 kilometres to go and fuel was running low. To add to their problems the airship ran into very 'bumpy' conditions over Nova Scotia.

On Sunday morning Major Scott decided that they would have to land and refuel before reaching New York. Major H. C. Fuller, who had arrived in New York by sea in order to organise the landing arrangements, heard the news and immediately rushed north to Boston to prepare for the refuelling stop. Then the wind changed to a steady following breeze which helped R34 on her way and made a stop unnecessary. At 9.20 a.m. she was over Mineola on Long Island, New York, but Major Fuller was not there to organise the ground crew – he was in Boston. An experienced officer was needed on the ground, so Major J. E. M. Pritchard on board the R34 had a quick shave, put on his parachute and jumped overboard. He wanted to look smart because he was going to be the first man to arrive in America by air. At 9.54 a.m. the R34 landed at

Mineola, having been in the air for 108 hours 12 minutes. She had only 140 gallons (about 636 litres) of petrol left, which would have lasted just another two hours.

The people in New York had been looking forward to the arrival of the R34 for some time because they had never seen a large rigid airship. Major Scott and his crew were overwhelmed with hospitality for three days, but they still had to fly back across the Atlantic and late on Wednesday 9th July the R34 departed from New York to a great cheer from the thousands of spectators on the ground. With a strong following wind the R34 was travelling at nearly 80 mph (about 128 kph). All went well for some time, but on Friday one engine broke down and could not be repaired. The engines needed regular servicing in flight and for the return journey two extra engineers were carried. Consequently one radio operator and the stowaway were left behind, but the kitten was allowed to fly home.

As the R34 approached Ireland early on Saturday morning Major Scott was ordered by radio to land at Pulham Airship Station in Norfolk instead of returning to East Fortune. Naturally the crew were very disappointed, because their families and friends would be waiting to welcome them at East Fortune. Major Scott asked if the order could be changed but his request was refused, and so on Sunday morning 13th July R34 landed safely at Pulham, 75 hours 3 minutes after leaving New York. The 11,000-kilometre flight was a great feat of endurance and established many records including the first flight from Europe to America and the first double crossing of the Atlantic.

11 The battered Wellingtons

During the Second World War many aircraft returned from missions despite being badly damaged, but one aircraft which earned an outstanding reputation for its ability to take punishment was the Vickers Wellington. In the RAF this twin-engined bomber was often nicknamed 'Wimpy', after the cartoon character J. Wellington Wimpy – Popeye's rather fat friend.

The story behind the Wellington's robust construction begins rather strangely, with an airship. In 1924 the Government ordered two new airships, the R100 and the R101. The Chief Engineer responsible for the design of the R100 was a young man with many original ideas, called Barnes Wallis (later to become Sir Barnes Wallis, whose inventions included the famous dam-busting bomb). For the R100 Barnes Wallis developed a new type of lattice-work or 'geodetic' construction which he used to make the basic framework of the airship. This framework was then covered with fabric to give the airship its streamlined shape. R100 made a successful flight to Canada and back in 1930, but shortly afterwards the R101 crashed and it was decided to scrap the R100.

Barnes Wallis joined Vickers Aviation at Weybridge in Surrey and started to adapt his geodetic structure for use in aeroplanes. At first sight the mass of criss-cross members seemed rather complex and the Air Ministry refused to support its development. Vickers had faith in Wallis and decided to build a long-range bomber using his ideas. This private venture was called the Wellesley, and it was such a success that the experts at the Air Ministry had to revise their opinion. Seventy-nine aircraft were ordered, and two of these broke the world long-distance record by flying non-stop from Egypt to Australia – a distance of 11,520 kilometres.

After the success of the Wellesley, Barnes Wallis and Vickers' Chief Designer Rex Pierson set about designing a twin-engined bomber and on 15th June, 1936 a gleaming new aircraft took off from the Brooklands aerodrome, around which ran the famous motor racing track. The new bomber did not have a name, so it was known by its specification number – B.9/32. It was just a short step from the B.9/32 to the Wellington Mark I which flew in December 1937 and was soon being produced in large numbers. Some people were critical of the Wellington's geodetic construction and said it was too complicated for mass-production. But Wallis and his colleagues tackled the problem and special tools were produced to make the work simple enough for semi-skilled workers. Vickers planned to build Wellingtons at the rate of one per day, and just to prove how simple it was they did actually build one Wellington in twenty-four hours, as a special exercise.

At first sight the Wellington seemed an old-fashioned aircraft, because its geodetic framework was covered with fabric, whereas most military aircraft were 'all-metal' (a light metal framework covered with a thin metal skin). It was sometimes referred to as 'the cloth bomber', but the rugged structure underneath the 'cloth' was the important part. An uncovered Wellington was a mass of lattice-work, the criss-cross members weaving an intricate pattern of squares and diamonds. If one, two or even more of these members were shot away, there were still plenty left to hold the aircraft together, but to do this the structure had to flex so that all the remaining members shared the load. This was the secret of the geodetic construction – it was flexible.

57

The Second World War started on 3rd September, 1939, and the following day fourteen Wellingtons were in action bombing two German warships. Unfortunately it was not a very effective raid, and two aircraft failed to return. Most of the early missions flown by Wellingtons were daylight raids against German shipping and naval bases. But it was soon discovered that bombers could not defend themselves against fighters in daylight, and the Wellingtons were transferred to night raids on industrial targets. In August 1940 Berlin was bombed for the first time, and in May 1942 Cologne was attacked by 1046 bombers – the first 'thousand-bomber' raid. During this period the Wellington was the backbone of Bomber Command.

There were many stories of Wellingtons returning to their home bases in a very battered condition. Some had gaping holes in the structure or large areas of fabric torn away, and it was jokingly suggested that a Wellington would fly without any fabric covering at all. One machine returned from a raid on Duisburg in April 1943 with the rear gunturret completely blown off and the rear fuselage stripped of fabric. Nevertheless the control surfaces on the tail unit were still working.

It was not always the aircraft which was the hero of the mission. Take, for example, the story of Sergeant J. A. Ward, a young New Zealander and member of a Wellington crew flying over the Zuider Zee. German fighters attacked and a fire started in one wing of the plane near the engine. The crew tried to put the fire out with extinguishers but it was too far away, so Sergeant Ward volunteered to climb out on to the wing and tackle the fire. Anyone who has put a hand out of the window of a car moving at 70 mph (113 kph) knows that the wind exerts quite a force, and climbing out of an aircraft flying at nearly 200 mph (322 kph) was not going to be easy. Ward tied a rope around his body and one of the crew held on to the other end, and he also wore his parachute just in case he got blown off the wing. Now, clambering about on the smooth surface of a wing is difficult as there are no hand-holds, and on an all-metal aircraft it would be almost impossible. But Sergeant Ward made small holes in the fabric and hung on to the geodetic structure underneath. He reached the fire and put it out, and then scrambled back into the fuselage. For this feat of courage he was awarded the Victoria Cross.

12 The wooden Mosquito

The people who joked about the Wellington being old-fashioned, with its fabric-covered structure, would have been even more astounded by the De Havilland Mosquito which first flew in 1940 – it was made of wood. Like the Wellington, it was a twin-engined bomber of the Second World War and carried a bomb load ranging from 900 to 1800 kilos. However, the speed of the two aircraft was very different – the Wellington had a top speed of about 250 mph (400 kph), but the Mosquito could fly at almost 400 mph (644 kph). Its speed and ability to fly at high altitudes made the Mosquito a very safe aircraft because enemy fighters could not intercept it.

News of the Mosquito was released to the public in September 1942, when four aircraft carried out a daring daylight raid on the Gestapo headquarters building in Oslo, Norway. But the Mosquito had been in service for a year by then, and its story begins in the early years of the war. The De Havilland Aircraft Company realised that aluminium was going to be in short supply because most military aircraft were built from aluminium and its alloys (aluminium with other metals added to produce a stronger 'alloy'). During the 1930s De Havillands had been building civil aircraft in wood, and they had developed a method of construction which was far removed from the old slab-sided framework covered with fabric. They still used a wooden framework but it was covered with thin plywood moulded to give a sleek and streamlined shape. This plywood skin added to the overall strength of the aircraft and it was better able to stand up to the air pressures and buffeting at high speeds. One of De Havilland's early high-speed wooden aircraft was their 'Comet' racer, built for the England-to-Australia air race in 1934. Despite very little test flying, a Comet reached Australia in 70 hours 59 minutes to win the race. A few years later De Havillands produced another fast, streamlined wooden aircraft – an airliner called the Albatross. Next they suggested a high-speed unarmed bomber, but the Ministry of Aircraft Production told them to drop the idea. Luckily the Ministry changed their minds in the early days of the war and work began on the Mosquito.

A wooden aeroplane had several advantages in addition to saving valuable aluminium. Plans were made to build Mosquitos not only in Britain but also in Australia and Canada where timber was plentiful and there were carpenters available to do the work. Carpenters could also be used to repair aircraft damaged during operations, and this was a great advantage because sheet-metal workers were needed for work on other aircraft. Finally, for air crews the wooden Mosquito had another great asset as it would often float for hours if brought down in the sea – it became its own lifeboat.

The designers of the Mosquito paid great attention to producing an aircraft with an outstanding performance, but they did not lose sight of the fact that it had to be built in large numbers by semi-skilled workers. Now, working inside a relatively small fuselage is always difficult because of the cramped conditions, so the Mosquito fuselage was made in two halves. The left side and the right side were made separately, then most of the equipment, pipes and wires were fitted before the two halves were joined together. Incidentally, these two shells were made of a wooden 'sandwich' material worked out for the Albatross airliner. This consisted of two sheets of thin plywood with a thick layer of balsa wood sandwiched between them and all glued together into a strong rigid shell. Balsa wood is very light and for this reason popular with builders of flying model aircraft, but it is not very strong. The thin plywood provided the strength while the balsa wood prevented this thin ply from buckling or wrinkling. The Mosquito's wing was constructed in one piece from tip to tip and built up using spruce with a plywood skin. Two Rolls-Royce Merlin engines were mounted on the wing to give the 'wooden wonder' the power it needed – after all it was claimed to be 'the fastest aircraft in operation in the world'.

Stories of the Mosquito in action would fill several books, but it was more than just an aircraft – it was a family of aircraft. Of the first fifty built, ten were photographic reconnaissance (P.R.) aircraft fitted with powerful cameras, thirty were fighters armed with four cannon plus four machine guns, and ten were bombers. Later in the war other versions were built including fighter-bombers with guns and bombs, mine-layers, rocket-carriers, pathfinders to lead heavy bombers to their target, and even Mosquito transport aircraft. The first Mosquito to fly an operational mission was one of the P.R. aircraft, which took photographs over Paris on 20th September, 1941. Early in 1942 the fighters and bombers went into action and were an immediate success.

Mosquito bombers were very effective against 'pinpoint' targets such as the Oslo Gestapo headquarters or the prison at Amiens which was attacked to allow captured Resistance fighters to escape. Power stations and railways were frequently attacked, and when the bomber version of the Mosquito was adapted to carry a 4000 lb 'block-buster' bomb (about 1800 kilos) it became even more devastating. Daring low-level attacks were made on railway tunnels in Germany, during which 4000 lb bombs were dropped right into the entrances. Another low-level attack was made on the Kiel Canal, and mines dropped into the busy waterway. Towards the end of the war, when the Germans were firing the V-1 flying bomb or 'Doodlebug' against the south of England, Mosquito bombers were sent to attack the launching sites and

were by far the most effective bomber for this work. Mosquito fighters played their part by shooting down 600 V-1s in two months, and were also used to attack enemy bombers and escort British bombers over Germany. However, the most widely used version of the Mosquito was the fighter-bomber. It was used as an 'intruder' to attack ground targets and generally harass the enemy on land and sea.

It is unusual to break records in wartime, but several Mosquitos built in Canada broke the North Atlantic record on their delivery flights, though the times had to be kept secret. Many of the Mosquito's transport services were also very secret. Important passengers, mail and vital cargo were carried to Moscow, Stockholm, Karachi and bases in Africa. When ball-bearings were in very short supply in Britain they were smuggled out of Sweden by Mosquitos – Sweden was not at war but was surrounded by German-held territory.

Following the success of the wooden Mosquito, De Havillands continued to use wood for their Hornet fighter of 1946. They even continued its use into the jet-age – both the Vampire and the Venom jet fighters had fuselages made of a plywood and balsa sandwich like the Mosquito.

13 Amy Johnson's flight to Australia

At 8 o'clock in the morning on Monday 5th May, 1930, a small De Havilland Gipsy Moth took off from Croydon Aerodrome and headed for Australia. The pilot was an unknown young woman from Hull in Yorkshire called Amy Johnson. The event did not attract any crowds or reporters – in fact the only people there to say 'goodbye' were Amy's father, a few officials and one or two friends from the London Aeroplane Club. Yet within a few days Amy Johnson was to become famous.

Amy went to school in Hull and then studied at Sheffield University, intending to become a teacher. Having obtained a degree, however, she decided to become a secretary with a London firm of solicitors. Her parents were interested in aviation without being enthusiasts – her mother had flown to Paris several times with Imperial Airways, and Amy herself had been on a five-shilling joy-ride over Hull. Her interest in flying grew and eventually she joined the Air League, doing voluntary work as a typist in the evenings.

Once she had saved enough money, Amy joined the London Aeroplane Club and learned to fly in her spare time. By June 1929 she qualified for her pilot's licence, but did not stop there – she had decided to try her hand at long-distance solo flying, and for this she needed to know about aero engines. When a girl asked to become a mechanic some eyebrows were raised, but the Chief Engineer at the Flying Club took her on and supervised her studies. Amy worked from 6 to 8.30 a.m., then rushed to her typing job, did a day's work and returned to the workshops in the evening. As she said, 'A hard life, but Jove – it's a good one.' Despite moving in a man's world, Amy remained very feminine and was a quiet but popular member of the Flying Club.

Thanks to her parents' help, Amy was able to buy a second-hand Gipsy Moth which had been fitted with a long-range fuel tank. She named her aircraft *Jason* and had it painted green, despite protests from friends who said that green was an unlucky colour. In fact she enjoyed not being superstitious and even bought a green flying suit, yet she was far from reckless and invested in a parachute just in case she had trouble in the air. Her one aim was to fly to Australia, and later she explained, 'Why I wanted to fly this particular route I really do not know, except that it was the greatest distance I could fly with a Gipsy Moth.' Most of the money needed to pay for the flight came from Amy's own hard-earned savings, but she could not raise enough and there was no prize to be won. Eventually Lord Wakefield of Hythe, who had helped many other aviators, offered to give her financial help. Now plans for the flight could go ahead, despite the fact that she had never flown across the Channel before, nor had she ever flown more than 320 kilometres in a straight line.

Amy's first objective was Vienna, 1300 kilometres from London, and after ten hours in the air she arrived safely. *Jason*'s cruising speed was about 85 mph (137 kph) and the little biplane could carry enough fuel for $13\frac{1}{2}$ hours' flying, or a range of 1822 kilometres. After a night's rest Amy left the next morning on another 1300-kilometre flight, this time to Constantinople. By now the newspapers were beginning to sense a story, and reports of her progress became news. On the third day she reached Aleppo, having flown a total of 3220 kilometres.

The next stage was one of only 800 kilometres, but involved

flying across the desert to Baghdad. A blinding sandstorm forced Amy to land and take shelter. For two hours she waited on the ground for the storm to pass, struggling to hold *Jason* down and keeping her revolver handy, just in case any unfriendly Arabs arrived on the scene. After this short but unpleasant break, she continued her flight to Baghdad and on to India. She reached Karachi in six days and broke the light plane record set up by Bert Hinkler, a very famous and experienced pilot. The newspapers were now getting very excited and Amy was front-page news. They asked: 'Will Amy Johnson beat Bert Hinkler's record of 15½ days to Australia?'

Amy was not out to break records – her target was just to reach Australia. Nevertheless she continued as speedily as she could across India to Calcutta, which was 11,270 kilometres from home and over half-way to Australia. She was still two days in front of Hinkler's time. The 1000-kilometre flight from Calcutta to Rangoon in Burma was a hazardous one, with jungles and a mountain range to contend with. Amy took *Jason* up to 3658 metres to cross the mountains but later very poor visibility forced her down to 46 metres, and she clung to the coastline hoping to follow the railway to Rangoon. Here the racecourse was to serve as a landing ground, but in a tropical downpour Amy could not find it and landed instead on the playing fields of an Engineering College, just outside the city. Unfortunately, *Jason* ran into a ditch and suffered considerable damage but, as Amy said: 'What better place could I have chosen!' The students made new parts and men's shirts were used to patch the damaged fabric of the wings.

Rather than risk taking off from the playing fields, Amy decided to transport *Jason* by road to the racecourse where the take-off run could be much longer. Two days had been lost, and after a short test flight she was on her way to Bangkok in Siam. Now this was only 573 kilometres away, which should have taken about four hours, but Amy had trouble crossing a range of mountains which were engulfed in thick clouds. She climbed to 3048 metres but still could not see anything, and

when a clear patch of sky did emerge she was still on the wrong side of the mountains. After seven hours she arrived at Bangkok, still level with Bert Hinkler's time, but exhausted.

The stage from Bangkok to Singapore was under 1500 kilometres and Amy hoped to make it in one hop, but strong headwinds slowed her down with the result that she had to make an overnight stop. This put Bert Hinkler's record beyond her reach, but nevertheless she was well on the way to her original goal, which was to reach Australia by air. In Singapore a new wing was fitted to *Jason* to replace the damaged one while Amy was given a meal and a well-deserved rest at the RAF officers' mess. From Singapore she set out for Sourabaya 1609 kilometres away and was well on the way when her fuel ran low. She landed at a sugar plantation and unfortunately some bamboo posts pierced *Jason*'s wings. These holes were repaired with pink sticking plaster! Amy reached Sourabaya the next day, but her engine was sounding a little rough. Early in the morning she was on her way again, aiming for an island to the north of Australia. The world waited for news but there was silence all day and all night. Search parties were on the point of setting out, when news came through that Amy was safe. She had landed at an isolated village, which did not have a telephone, a mere twenty kilometres from her objective.

On 24th May, 1930, which was appropriately Empire Day, Amy set out on the last stage of her 16,000-kilometre journey. This involved crossing the dreaded shark-infested Timor Sea, but for once Amy had no problems and reached Port Darwin early in the afternoon. This first solo flight to Australia by a woman was greeted by loud cheers from an excited crowd. Amy Johnson had left Croydon as an unknown girl pilot, but 19½ days later she was a world-famous figure.

14 By airline to South Africa – 1932 style

Today it is possible to fly to South Africa from London in a matter of twelve hours, but in 1932 it was a very different story – in fact it might well be described as an adventure story. The 13,000-kilometre journey took almost twelve days and involved about thirty stops, but a modern jet airliner can make the flight without a single stop. Air mail services to South Africa were introduced in January 1932 by the British airline Imperial Airways, and a few months later they carried passengers for the first time.

Imagine we are passengers on one of those flights. We must be at Victoria Station at 11.45 a.m. on any Wednesday morning, complete with our tropical clothing, for later we shall be crossing the Equator. The train takes us to Croydon Aerodrome, where we arrive soon after noon and proceed with the formalities familiar to all air travellers – the ticket check, baggage weighing, Customs inspection and passport examination. Croydon Aerodrome is much smaller than modern airports and our airliner is standing just outside the main building on the 'tarmac' – there are no runways, just a grass field. It is a very large biplane with two engines on the upper wing and two on the lower. The name on the nose is *Helena*, and it is one of Imperial Airways' most reliable airliners – a Handley Page H.P.42. It is due to take off at 12.30 for Paris, on the regular London-to-Paris service travellers to South Africa have to use for the first stage of their long journey.

We climb aboard and sit in one of the thirty-eight comfortable armchairs. The engines start up, the airliner taxis out to the field, and after a very short run it is airborne. As we cross the Channel at a steady 100 mph (about 160 kph) we eat our four-course lunch. We arrive in Paris at about 2.15 p.m. with time to look around before the next stage of the journey starts from the Gare de Lyon railway station at 10.30 p.m. Imperial Airways are not allowed to take us any further through France or Italy because of a European agreement which allows only local airlines to operate within their own country. Consequently we have to travel by train for two nights and a day in order to reach Brindisi in the south of Italy, where we arrive early on Friday morning. Luckily there are sleeping cars on the train!

At 10.15 a.m. we board an Imperial Airways Short Kent four-engined flying boat and take off from the sea on our way to Athens. We cross the Adriatic Sea and see Mount Olympus before landing in the Greek capital at tea-time. The night is spent in Athens, but we have to be up early ready to leave again at 6 a.m. Our flying boat lands at Mirabella on the island of Crete to refuel, and then it flies across the Mediterranean Sea to Alexandria in Egypt. After landing in the early afternoon, a train takes us to Cairo where an early night is recommended as the airline favours early morning departures. We leave Cairo aerodrome early on Sunday morning, flying in an Armstrong-Whitworth Argosy three-engined biplane. This is one of Imperial Airways' older airliners – in fact it was one of the first really successful commercial airliners, built in 1926. From Cairo we fly south along the River Nile and see some of the famous sights of Egypt such as the Pyramids and the Valley of the Kings. The Argosy has to land twice to refuel during the day, and by evening we have arrived at Wadi Halfa in the Sudan. On Monday we are allowed an extra hour or so in bed as the Argosy does not depart until 8 a.m.

After one refuelling stop the Argosy lands at Khartoum where we are to spend the night.

Once again we change aircraft and return to a flying boat as there are plenty of lakes ahead but no aerodromes. On Tuesday morning at 5 a.m. we take off from the River Nile in a graceful Short Calcutta, which has three engines mounted between its wings. Our Calcutta flies towards Juba at a steady 90 mph (about 145 kph), passing over inhospitable-looking jungle. One flying boat did have to make a forced landing in this area, and its seventeen passengers had to wait for a couple of days to be rescued. A report said, 'They passed a not un-interesting, if somewhat unpleasant, time, and towards the end food supplies were running short; at night the mosquitoes were very troublesome.' Our flight has no problems, and after two stops we arrive in Juba and retire to bed. So ends the first week of our journey.

On Wednesday morning we take off in the flying boat once again. After a refuelling stop we cross the Equator and land on Lake Victoria at Kisumu. After disembarking we transfer to yet another land plane – an old De Havilland D.H.66 Hercules biplane which has three engines and looks rather like the Argosy. It takes off from a nearby aerodrome and flies on to Nairobi in Kenya, which is our overnight stopping place. Soon after take-off in the morning we can see the impressive sight of Mount Kilimanjaro, which is Africa's highest mountain and a useful landmark for pilots as it is sometimes visible from 150 kilometres away.

Now we have to spend four days in the Hercules flying across the hills and high plains of southern Africa with overnight stops at M'beya by Lake Nyasa, Salisbury in Rhodesia and Johannesburg in the Transvaal. The Hercules was built in 1926 and it was not designed to operate in these hot conditions, nor from aerodromes such as Nairobi or Johannesburg which are both over 1500 metres above sea-level. Imperial Airways hope to introduce their new Armstrong-Whitworth Atalanta monoplane airliner on this route by the end of the year, but in the meantime our Hercules gets us to Cape Town on Sunday evening. Table Mountain and the blue waters of Table Bay are a very welcome sight to travellers who have just spent twelve days either in the air or on a train, but we have beaten the fastest mail boat – it takes about seventeen days!

Our imaginary flight covered 13,000 kilometres in twelve days and eleven nights – an overall average speed of under 30 mph (50 kph). Gradually Imperial Airways speeded up their service, and the introduction of the Atalanta helped by cutting two days off the schedule. When the new long-range Short Empire flying boats entered service in 1937, the journey time was cut to $6\frac{1}{2}$ days and then to $4\frac{1}{2}$ in the following year.

15 The first jet engine?

Who built the first jet engine? Well, there is no easy answer, because it all depends on what is meant by 'jet engine'. For instance, in 1729 an English inventor called Dr John Allen suggested a jet-propelled boat but he did not build one. In 1787 an American engineer, James Rumsey, actually built a jet-propelled boat, powered by a steam engine which pumped a jet of water out of the stern. This method of propulsion was not a success, and anyway it hardly qualifies as a jet engine because to most people a jet engine means the type of engine used to power today's airliners, fighters and bombers. The modern jet engine belongs to a whole family of engines called 'gas turbines'.

In a gas turbine, air is drawn into the engine and compressed by an air compressor, then it passes to a combustion section into which fuel is sprayed and ignited. The fuel burns fiercely and produces hot gases at a high temperature and pressure. These gases emerge from the rear of the engine as a jet. However, before emerging they pass through a turbine (a high-speed windmill), and this turbine drives the compressor. If a larger turbine is fitted it can be used to drive a propeller in addition to the compressor, and this is called a turbo-prop or prop-jet engine. When the gas turbine was first introduced in 1905, it was not intended for use in aircraft but as an industrial engine. Most of the power from its hot gases was absorbed by a large turbine which drove machinery. Consequently it became known as a gas turbine to distinguish it from the steam turbine which had been in use for some years. The hot gases were quite a problem because, in the early days, there were no metals which could stand up to their heat.

The story of the aircraft jet engine starts during the 1930s in Britain and Germany, where very secret and quite separate experiments were being carried out. Britain won the race to design, build and test-run a jet engine on the ground, but Germany was the first to fly a jet aircraft. In Britain the leading figure was a Flying Instructor in the RAF called Frank Whittle (later to become Sir Frank Whittle). The idea of adapting the gas turbine engine to power an aircraft seemed a logical development to Whittle, and in 1929 he tried to persuade the Air Ministry that his engine was feasible. They turned it down. Nevertheless, he patented the design in January 1930 and then concentrated on his flying career. A few years later Whittle went to Cambridge University to study engineering and carry out research. A new company called Power Jets Ltd was set up to help Whittle develop his jet engine, and work began in earnest. By 1937 Whittle and his colleagues from Power Jets had built the world's first jet engine, and on 12th April it was run for the first time in a 'test bed'.

In Germany a young engineer called Hans Pabst von Ohain had also been working on a jet engine in collaboration with the well known aircraft designer Professor Ernst Heinkel, and in September 1937 von Ohain's engine ran for the first time. Heinkel had already built an aeroplane powered by a rocket motor, so the job of producing an aeroplane powered by a jet engine was no great problem. On 27th August, 1939, test pilot Erich Warsitz climbed into the cockpit of the diminutive Heinkel He 178, started the noisy engine and took off. The jet age had started. But it ended again almost immediately, for when the Second World War began only a few days later,

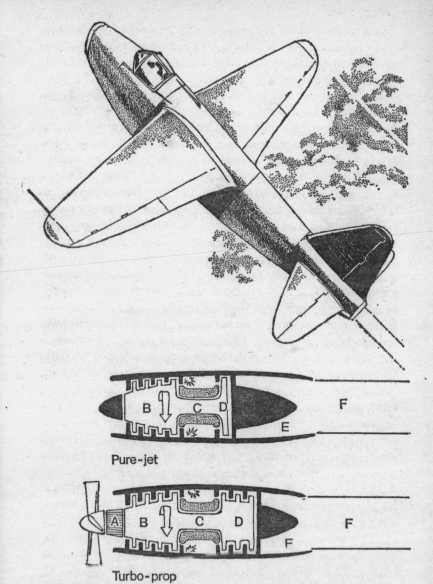

Pure-jet

Turbo-prop

A gearbox. B compressor. C combustion chamber. D turbine.
E jet-pipe. F jet.

Hitler stopped the test-flying of both the rocket and jet aircraft. He wanted all the aircraft industry's effort put into the production of existing designs in the hope of winning the war as quickly as possible.

In Italy, however, research was being encouraged, and exactly one year after the Heinkel's flight their 'jet' aircraft made its first flight. It was called the Caproni-Campini C.C.2 (or N.1 sometimes) and it certainly looked like a jet aircraft – but was it? The Italians claimed it was, and amidst great publicity it made a cross-country flight from Milan to Rome, with a stop at Pisa to refuel. The design was the work of an engineer called Secondo Campini, and the aircraft was built by the Caproni Company of Milan. It was propelled by a jet of air coming out of the rear fuselage, but it did not have a gas turbine engine. An ordinary piston engine was used – just like the engine of any propeller-driven aeroplane – but the engine of the C.C.2. drove three small propellers which were fitted inside a tunnel running the length of the fuselage. Just before the air emerged from the tunnel, fuel was sprayed into the airstream and burnt. This gave extra thrust and the idea was later used on conventional jet engines when it became known as an 'afterburner'. The C.C.2 was not as fast as had been hoped, and even flat out could only reach 230 mph (370 kph), which was slower than some of the old biplanes! To make matters worse it was consuming fuel at an alarming rate, hence the stop to refuel on its relatively short flight from Milan to Rome. After about two years spent on research, there was little improvement and the project was abandoned.

Meanwhile, in Britain Air Ministry officials saw Whittle's jet engine running in its test bed, and although they were still a little apprehensive they gave financial support. In March 1938 an order was placed for a new engine to power an experimental aircraft specially designed to take the new jet engine. This aircraft was called the Gloster E.28/39, and it made its first flight on 15th May, 1941 with Flight Lieutenant P. E. G. Sayer at the controls, although it had made a very short hop previously during taxiing trials. The engine on this historic flight was a Whittle W.1 fitted with a centrifugal air compressor, ten combustion chambers and a turbine to drive the compressor. Both aircraft and engine are preserved in the Science Museum in London. As tests continued they demonstrated that the jet engine became more efficient at high speeds and greater altitudes, whereas the conventional piston engine became less efficient under these conditions. These facts had been Whittle's argument from the beginning, but it had been a long struggle to overcome both the technical difficulties and the lack of interest in some official circles.

The first aeroplane to fly using a jet engine was undoubtedly the German Heinkel He 178 in August 1939, some two years before Whittle's first engine was ready for flight testing. However, the Heinkel's engine was not developed for production aircraft, whereas many of the early British and American jet aircraft were powered by engines based on Whittle's design.

16 Faster than sound

Flying at a speed faster than the speed of sound means that the aircraft arrives before its noise, and to do this it has to break through the so-called 'sound barrier'.

Of course we now know that there is no real barrier, but fighter pilots at the end of the Second World War did run into trouble when they dived their aircraft at very high speeds. As they approached the speed of sound they were severely buffeted and the trim (or balance) of their aircraft changed suddenly. Sometimes these strange effects were so serious that the aircraft broke up in the air or the pilot completely lost control. When the newspapers heard about these mysterious accidents, the reporters made the most of the 'sound barrier' theory. A barrier is not a very good description – for instance, a high wall is a barrier to a walker, but a muddy field just slows him down because the going is heavy. Now, reaching the speed of sound is more like the muddy field, because the drag on the aircraft suddenly increases. Shock waves are formed and these can be heard on the ground as a 'sonic boom'.

The pilots who ran into trouble were not always aware how near to the speed of sound they were getting, because this critical speed varies with height. At sea level the speed of sound is about 1220 kph and it gradually decreases to 1060 kph at 11,000 metres. From this height upwards it stays at 1060 kph. These changes make it rather difficult to keep track of the all-important speed of sound, so instead of measuring the air-craft's speed in kilometres per hour it is measured by com-parison with the speed of sound, which is called Mach 1. This name honours the Austrian scientist Ernst Mach who studied the behaviour of sound waves. An aircraft flying at twice the speed of sound is said to be flying at Mach 2, and this speed is indicated on a mach-meter. Despite the predictions by sci-entists and aerodynamicists about what would happen when an aircraft reached Mach 1, no one could really be sure. Usually advanced new designs for aircraft were tried out by making a model and testing it in a wind tunnel, but the shock waves at Mach 1 made this kind of test unreliable. The first man to fly faster than sound would be following in the footsteps of the pioneers of aviation who ventured into the unknown.

During 1945 an aeroplane designed to fly faster than sound was being built in the United States. It had been ordered jointly by the U.S. Air Force and a Government research organisation, and the builders were the Bell Aircraft Cor-poration. The Bell X-1 was a very simple-looking aeroplane with a bullet-like fuselage and small thin wings. In the rear of the fuselage four small but powerful rocket motors were fitted and these could be fired one at a time or all together. At full power their fuel lasted only a few minutes. On 19th January, 1946, the X-1 made its first flight but there was no spectacular take-off – it was carried into the air by a Boeing B-29 Superfortress and allowed to glide back to its base. In-cidentally, Edwards Air Force Base in California has been described as 'Nature's gift to the Air Force' because it con-sists of a dried-out lake eighteen kilometres long and eleven wide. The hard clay surface stretching for kilometre after kilometre makes an ideal natural runway for aircraft like the X-1, which landed at 170 mph (about 274 kph). The American test programme continued cautiously with more gliding flights, then in December 1946 the second X-1 was carried into the air and during its glide the rocket motors were fired for the first time. Nearly another year passed before an X-1 was ready to try for Mach 1.

The pilot selected to fly the X-1 was Air Force Captain Charles E. Yeager – Chuck to his friends. He named his aircraft *Glamorous Glennis* after his wife, but officially it was number 6062. On 14th October, 1947, Charles Yeager climbed through the small door in the side of his cockpit and prepared for take-off. The huge B-29 carried the X-1 to a high altitude and released it. Yeager started his engines and levelled out at 42,000 feet (about 12,800 metres). He increased the power of his rocket motors and the speed of the X-1 built up rapidly until Mach 1 was reached – then exceeded. Yeager's speed in level flight was Mach 1.015 or 670 mph (1078 kph), at a height where the speed of sound was 660 mph (1062 kph). At last man had been able to prove there was no 'sound barrier', and the cautious preparations had ensured that Yeager could control the X-1 as it went supersonic. Chuck Yeager did not become famous overnight – in fact news of his flight was not released officially for another eight months.

The research programme into supersonic flight continued and improved versions of the X-1 were designed. In June 1954 Yeager reached a speed of Mach 2.42 in the X-1A. But these aircraft were rocket-powered flying laboratories, and it was some time before supersonic aircraft were ready for military service.

In Britain the first aircraft to exceed the speed of sound was a De Havilland D.H.108, unofficially called the Swallow. This was a small, tailless research aircraft powered by a jet engine, and when it approached Mach 1 it became difficult to control. On 6th September, 1948, test pilot John Derry took off intending to reach Mach 0.96. The Swallow could only achieve about Mach 0.85 in level flight, so John Derry had to put it into a dive to reach his target. As the speed built up the controls became ineffective, and Derry found himself in a vertical dive with the speed building up to Mach 0.97, then

1.00. He throttled back the engine but his speed still increased to Mach 1.04. He operated the small flaps, normally used to trim the aircraft, and they worked very gradually, pulling the Swallow out of its dive. Flying at the speed of sound could still present problems.

The first supersonic aircraft to enter service was the North American F-100A Super Sabre jet fighter built for the United States Air Force. The first prototype flew in May 1953 and this was closely followed by aircraft intended for squadron service, but once again there was trouble with the controls in the region of Mach 1 and changes had to be made. Once these problems had been solved the Super Sabre became a very successful aircraft capable of 1240 kph at sea level (or, to be more correct, Mach 1.01).

17 From scouts to fighters

Only eleven years after man-carrying balloons had been invented, they were pressed into military service as lookout posts. Balloons filled with the light gas hydrogen were used and in their baskets they carried a pilot and an observer armed with a telescope. These balloons were not set free, otherwise they would have drifted away: instead they were attached by a rope to the ground and flown rather like a kite. From this high look-out post an observer could spy on enemy troops and send signals down to his own forces.

The first military observation balloon was made by the French in 1794, shortly after the Revolution which ended the rule of King Louis XVI. It was first tried out at Maubeuge for observing enemy troops from Austria and Holland who were positioned just outside the town. But this particular balloon had an even greater triumph a few weeks later on 26th June, 1794, at the Battle of Fleurus. A French General ascended in the balloon and for about ten hours he directed operations from above. Written messages were lowered down or hauled up by the high-flying General. But the presence of the balloon had another effect on the battle, as most of the Austrian troops had never seen a balloon before and a rumour spread that the French were in league with the devil. The Austrians were thoroughly disheartened and the French won a great victory – the first battle in which air power played an important part.

History has a strange way of repeating itself and this is what happened when the aeroplane was invented. Eleven years after the Wright brothers' first flight, the First World War broke out and aeroplanes became look-out posts for the armies – like the balloon 120 years earlier. Of course aircraft had several advantages over balloons, because they could fly right over the enemy lines and they were much more difficult to shoot down from the ground. Observation balloons were still used, but they had to be kept some way back from the front lines and the dangers of enemy gunfire. The army commanders had two tasks to be carried out in the air. One was 'spotting' for their guns, which meant observing where the shells were landing and then signalling instructions to the gunners which helped them to hit their targets. Balloons were used for this work together with slow reconnaissance aircraft such as the two-seater B.E.2c designed at the Royal Aircraft Factory, Farnborough. The army's other job for aeroplanes was to make reconnaissance flights behind the enemy lines to see what the opposing troops were doing. Faster aircraft were used for this work and they were called 'scouts' as the army commanders thought of them as an aerial version of the old cavalry scout. Guns were not fitted to any of these aircraft, for the authorities had said there was 'no great likelihood of aerial scouts coming into conflict' – how wrong they were!

Britain had two very useful fast single-seater scouts in service with the Royal Flying Corps during 1914 – the Bristol Scout and the Sopwith Tabloid. Both were small biplanes capable of about 100 mph (160 kph) and the Tabloid had made a name for itself already by winning the second Schneider Trophy race just before the war started. Neither aircraft was armed, but the pilots usually carried a rifle or revolver just in case they met an enemy scout. One of the most popular French scouts of this time was the Morane-Saulnier Type L, which was a monoplane with its wing mounted above the fuselage –

an arrangement which gave the pilot an unobscured view of the ground. This 'parasol' wing scout was so successful that the Germans built copies of it and these were called Pfalz A1s, but the Germans had another scout monoplane in service designed by the Dutch aircraft designer Anthony Fokker. As the war continued the military experts realised that enemy reconnaissance flights had to be prevented if possible. Scout pilots were sent up to intercept the enemy aircraft, but it was very difficult to hit a moving target with a rifle. Machine guns were sometimes fitted but they had to be positioned at an awkward angle in order to avoid hitting their own propeller, for all these scouts had their engines in the nose of the aircraft.

A new era of aerial warfare began on 1st April, 1915, when a French pilot took off in his Morane-Saulnier Type L scout. The pilot, Roland Garros, had fitted a machine-gun to the nose of his aircraft just in front of the cockpit so that the gun could fire forwards. This enabled him to aim the gun by flying his aircraft straight towards the enemy. Of course the problem was to prevent the bullets from shooting away his own propeller, and he did this by bolting small steel wedges to the propeller blades just in line with the barrel of the gun. These wedges protected the propeller by deflecting away any bullets which did happen to hit it. It was rather a dangerous device, but on his first patrol with the machine gun Garros shot down a German two-seater reconnaissance aircraft. Several successes followed but a few weeks later Garros had to make a forced landing behind the enemy lines. The Germans captured his forward-firing machine-gun and ordered copies to be made. However, the German engineers and Anthony Fokker went a stage further and produced an aeroplane fitted with a forward-firing machine-gun which did not need dangerous deflector plates. The mechanism which actually fired the bullets was connected to the engine in such a way that it operated only when the propeller blades were not in the direct line of fire.

A Fokker monoplane was fitted with this new 'interrupter

gear', and in July 1915 the 'Fokker Scourge' began. The combination of this manoeuvrable monoplane with its forward-firing machine-gun made it far superior to any other fighting aircraft. British and French machines were hopelessly outclassed and for several months the Germans ruled the air. No interrupter gear was available for the British and French aircraft designers, so they had to find other solutions to combat the dreaded Fokker. The French mounted a machine-gun above the upper wing of their Nieuport biplane scout, and in this position it fired over the top of the rotating propeller. The British solution was to turn back the pages of history and reintroduce 'pusher' biplanes in which the engine was fitted to the rear of a short fuselage (so that it pushed, rather than pulled, the aircraft along). The tail unit had to be carried by a spidery arrangement of struts and wires. One of the most successful 'pushers' was the De Havilland D.H.2 single-seater. As the engine was situated behind the pilot, a forward-firing machine-gun could easily be fitted in the nose of the aircraft just in front of the cockpit. This was a very convenient position, not only for aiming but also for reloading – much better than the Nieuport's wing-mounted gun. But on the other hand the pusher design resulted in more air-resistance or 'drag' from all the struts and wires. D.H.2s reached British squadrons in France early in 1916 and quickly showed that they were superior to the Fokker monoplanes.

By 1916 the British and French had developed interrupter gears so they were able to fit forward-firing machine-guns to aeroplanes with a propeller at the front. Both sides were now building aircraft specifically designed to fight, and although the fighter aircraft had emerged from the scout, the old name stuck for some time. Monoplanes, biplanes and triplanes were tried, as were single- or two-seaters. By the end of the war the single-seater biplane with two machine-guns firing through the propeller emerged as the most successful fighter layout and remained so until the Second World War.

18 Malta's Gladiators

The Gloster Gladiator was one of the few biplane fighters to be used in action during the Second World War. In appearance it was not very different from the biplane fighters of the First World War, and as originally designed it even carried the same armament – two machine guns firing through the propeller. However, by the time the first aircraft was ready to fly two more guns had been added under the lower wings and clear of the propeller. The Gladiator made its first flight in September 1934 with Flight Lieutenant P. E. G. Sayer at the controls. Incidentally, only seven years later Gerry Sayer flew the Gloster-Whittle E.28/39 for the first time, and so he had the distinction of making two unique maiden flights – Britain's last biplane fighter and her first jet aircraft. By 1937 Gladiators were serving in the Royal Air Force as front-line fighters but, with a top speed of 250 mph (400 kph), their service life would be fairly limited because new monoplane fighters capable of well over 300 mph (480 kph) were being designed and built.

By the time war broke out in 1939, the RAF was receiving Hawker Hurricanes and Supermarine Spitfires, so the Gladiators were gradually being replaced. Nevertheless, two squadrons equipped with Gladiators were sent to fight in France during the early months of 1940. Although they were much slower than the German Messerschmitts, the Gladiators were extremely manoeuvrable and pilots of these sturdy little biplanes shot down a considerable number of enemy aircraft before the advance of the German army forced them to burn their aircraft and escape to Britain. Meanwhile, in Norway, Gladiators were also fighting against superior German forces and under very difficult conditions. Their runways were usually frozen lakes and their ground crews had to service the aircraft in the open air, despite the arctic weather.

Gladiators and Sea Gladiators (the naval version) fought on almost every battle-front during the early years of the war, but their most famous exploit was probably the defence of Malta. The island of Malta and its little neighbour Gozo are situated in the middle of the Mediterranean Sea at the crossroads of two vital sea routes. British ships needed to travel on the east-west route to supply their forces in Egypt, while German and Italian ships had to use the north-south route to link their forces in Italy and Libya. Italy had entered the war early in June 1940 at a time when Britain was in great danger. France had collapsed and the Germans were planning an invasion across the English Channel. Despite these threats at home, the defence of Malta and its British naval base was vitally important. The Royal Navy had warships in the Mediterranean to repel an attack from the sea, but the Italian Air Force was a real threat. The only Royal Air Force aircraft stationed at Malta were several old reconnaissance flying boats!

Everyone agreed that Malta needed fighters, but with the Battle of Britain about to start it was very difficult to find any Spitfires or Hurricanes which were not already overworked. However, in Malta's dockyard store there were some crates containing dismantled Sea Gladiators and spare parts. These had been in the store for some time as they were intended for the aircraft carrier *HMS Glorious* when she was based in the Indian Ocean. In the meantime, *Glorious* had been transferred to Norway, where she was sunk on 7th June, 1940, while evacuating the Gladiator squadrons after their operations from the frozen lakes. The RAF personnel on Malta opened the crates and set about assembling the Gladiators. They managed to get four aircraft ready to fly, but there were only a few pilots on the island including those from the flying boats and they had little or no experience of flying single-seater fighters. Two more Gladiators were assembled and one or two more pilots arrived, including one Fleet Air Arm pilot who had actually flown Gladiators. So, when Italy declared war, Malta had an air force of six Gladiators and seven pilots.

The Italian bombers came to test Malta's defences and the Gladiators went into action. Usually two, three or four took off, leaving one or two in reserve. When the Italians found that there were fighters on Malta after all, they decided to send fighters along to escort their bombers. The Gladiators were outnumbered, so their tactics were to attack the bombers as they approached the target area and make accurate bombing as difficult as possible – they did not want to become involved in long dog-fights with the Italians. During the early raids the local people refused to leave their homes, but as the attacks continued they had to take shelter in Malta's maze of underground tunnels and fortifications. Some of these old tunnels were hewn out of the rock by galley slaves centuries earlier, for Malta had experienced many sieges in its turbulent history.

Several enemy aircraft were shot down by the faithful Gladiators, but their age soon began to tell and rarely were all six in flying condition at any one time. Their Bristol Mercury engines were being strained to the limit – and beyond – by the pilots in an effort to reach the bombers before they could drop any bombs. Two Gladiators were grounded with worn-out engines, but there was on the island a Bristol Blenheim bomber which had also been grounded and it was fitted with two Mercury engines. With great ingenuity the RAF mechanics adapted the Blenheim's engines to fit the two Gladiators and get them back into the air. One of the pilots decided to fit two extra machine guns to his aircraft, but it was destroyed on the ground by enemy action. Then, over a period of a few

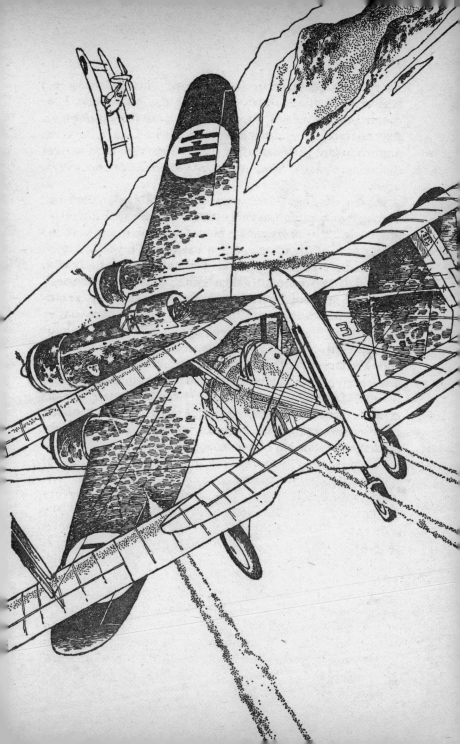

days, three Gladiators were damaged during landing or taxiing accidents which left only two in flying condition. The date was 26th June, 1940, and things looked bad, but two days later four Hurricanes arrived on Malta. Others followed and gradually the Gladiators were withdrawn from active service, having played an important part in the defence of the island.

During wartime, stories were sometimes exaggerated by over-enthusiasm, and at other times they were deliberately altered because propaganda played an important part in raising or lowering morale. Some accounts of the Gladiator's exploits were rather exaggerated at the time when it was claimed that three aircraft called 'Faith', 'Hope' and 'Charity' fought the might of the Italian Air Force day after day. There was really no need to exaggerate the part played by the Gladiators because they did two very important jobs. If they had not been there, then the Italians would undoubtedly have launched heavier attacks much sooner. When these heavier attacks did come, the Hurricanes had arrived to take over the defence. The second achievement of the Gladiators was to raise the morale of the Maltese people by letting them see that they were not going to be bombed without a fight – even if the fighters were slow old biplanes.

19 Forty years in service – the DC-3 story

The Douglas DC-3 is a twin-engined airliner which has carried passengers and cargo in almost every country of the world over a period of forty years and more – not surprisingly it became one of the best-known aircraft of all time.

This aircraft has been given many names and numbers – both official and unofficial – over the years, but it started life as the DC-3 in 1935. It was designed and built by the Douglas Aircraft Company of California, and the DC stood for Douglas Commercial. An early version equipped with sleeping accommodation was known as the DST (Douglas Sleeper Transport). The United States Army Air Corps ordered several military transport versions of which the C-47 Skytrain was the most widely used, while the variant used by the US Navy was known as the R4D. But these official titles were very often ignored by U.S. servicemen, who called it the 'Gooney Bird' – a nickname it shared with a quaint seabird found on some Pacific islands. The Royal Air Force also flew the DC-3 (or C-47) and called it the Dakota, but this was often shortened to the 'Dak' by RAF crews.

In Russia the DC-3 was known as the Lisunov Li-2, and during the Second World War 2000 to 3000 were built in Russian factories. The Japanese also built DC-3s during the war and their 500 aircraft caused considerable confusion in the Pacific area, because the same type of aircraft was being flown by both sides! Aircraft recognition from a distance was a problem at the best of times, but the DC-3 situation led to several tragic mistakes. When the war ended DC-3 airliners again began to roll off the production lines despite the fact that the design was, by then, ten years old.

The DC-3 story really begins with the DC-1 and its great rival, the Boeing 247. In February 1933 the Boeing 247 made its first flight and caused quite a sensation by carrying ten passengers at 155 mph (250 kph). Most of the 247's rivals cruised at about 100 mph (160 kph), but they were fairly cumbersome fabric-covered biplanes with fixed wheels whereas the Boeing 247 was a sleek all-metal monoplane with a retractable undercarriage. It represented a new era in airliner design. United Air Lines ordered sixty and by March 1933 the first 247s were introduced on their service across the United States. By cutting the journey time from twenty-seven to twenty hours the Boeing 247 attracted passengers from other airlines and this worried United's rivals, especially TWA (Transcontinental and Western Air, later to become Trans World Airlines). TWA tried to order 247s, but Boeings were too busy with the United order so TWA approached the Douglas Company and asked them to produce an airliner to rival the 247. Work started on the DC-1, which was something like the 247 in appearance but was soon found to be over-weight and underpowered. Luckily a more powerful engine became available, and this was fitted with a new type of pro-peller which gave the DC-1 a cruising speed of 170 mph (275 kph). Douglas decided to lengthen the fuselage slightly and increase the number of seats from twelve to fourteen. TWA immediately ordered the longer aircraft, which became the DC-2.

The DC-2 began to carry passengers in July 1934 and soon established itself as the most advanced passenger aircraft in the world. This fact was demonstrated later in the year during the England-to-Australia air race. The winner was a De Havilland Comet racer – forerunner of the wartime Mosquito

– but the second aircraft in the race was a standard DC-2 entered by the Dutch airline KLM and in third place was its great rival, a Boeing 247. The DC-2 even carried a few passengers, and on one occasion it had to re-land after leaving one behind on the ground. The DC-2 reached Australia in 3 days 18 hours, beating the Boeing by nearly three hours, but both airliners beat many special racing aircraft. About 220 DC-2s were eventually built and used in America, Europe, Australia and China.

Another United States airline was in trouble by this time, because it was still flying old biplanes which were unable to compete with the Boeing 247s and Douglas DC-2s. American Airlines decided that they needed a larger version of the DC-2 suitable for use on their important sleeper service across America. The fuselage of the DC-2 was too narrow to take sleeping berths so the DC-3 was born. For night flying, the new Douglas Sleeper Transport could provide berths for fourteen people, whereas a standard daytime version could seat twenty-one passengers. The first DC-3 flew on 17th December, 1935, and by June 1936 American Airlines introduced them on their busy New York-to-Chicago route. In September of the same year they introduced the sleeper version on their New York-to-Los Angeles service with a journey time of sixteen to eighteen hours. The DC-3 could cruise at 170–180 mph (about 275–290 kph), but perhaps more important was its reliability. It developed into one of the most dependable aircraft ever built, and this fact helped the airlines to introduce services which ran on time.

In the years before the Second World War many of the world's major airlines ordered the DC-3, and it became a familiar sight at most airports. As the war drew nearer General 'Hap' Arnold of the US Army Air Corps became convinced that the armed forces would need a large number of transport aircraft and he decided that the DC-3 was the ideal aircraft. Several examples were modified for military service, then in September 1940 the Army Air Corps ordered a new

strengthened version of the DC-3 with a large cargo door and a reinforced floor. This was the C-47, which could carry twenty-four troops plus their equipment or a load of military cargo including guns and vehicles. The Gooney Birds came to Britain in 1942, and during the war they were used for many different operations in addition to their main role as a military transport. They dropped paratroops and their supplies, towed gliders, transported important passengers and served as air ambulances. They were so successful that about ten thousand were built by the end of the war.

When peace returned, fewer military freighters were required, and hundreds of surplus C-47s were converted back to DC-3 airliners. This supply of cheap aircraft helped many airlines to start passenger services in the difficult days following the war. As these airlines became more prosperous they were able to buy new airliners, and the DC-3s were sold to smaller airlines carrying passengers and cargo in remote areas. The DC-3 became a real work-horse, carrying anything and everything from cattle to tomatoes. Some aircraft were modified for unusual jobs such as fire-fighting, crop spraying, planting seeds or searching the earth's surface for valuable minerals.

In 1975, forty years after the DC-3 first appeared, examples were still to be found flying on the routes of no less than 132 airlines. In fact there were still over four hundred DC-3s in service – far more than most of the airliners designed as a DC-3 replacement. One of the oldest DC-3s has been preserved in the National Air and Space Museum in the United States. This particular aircraft served with Eastern Airlines from 1937 to 1952 and completed 56,782 flying hours, which represents six and a half years spent in the air!

20 Admiral Byrd's Polar flights

Even before the first aeroplane flew, an attempt was made to reach the North Pole by air, for in the year 1897 a Swedish engineer, Salomon Andrée, set out with two companions in a large balloon. Their aim was to drift across the ice to the Pole, which meant they had to rely upon the wind blowing in the right direction. At first all went well, but unfortunately the wind changed and later the balloon crashed due to the weight of ice which formed on its surface. The three explorers set out on the long trek back to civilisation, but after two and a half months they perished. Their final camp was discovered 33 years later, and in it were their diaries and equipment including several films from their camera. Experts developed the films very carefully and were delighted to see pictures emerge. These included scenes of the crash and the overland journey.

In 1911 the famous Norwegian explorer Roald Amundsen became the first man to reach the South Pole overland, when he beat Captain Scott by a few weeks. Then in 1925 Amundsen decided to attempt a flight to the North Pole using two German Dornier Wal flying boats. Bad weather forced both aircraft to land on the sea before they had travelled very far, and after many days of hardship the two crews managed to escape in one of the Dorniers. However, Amundsen did not give up his hopes of flying to the North Pole, and made plans for a new expedition in the following year using an Italian

airship. In the meantime another expedition was being prepared by Lieutenant-Commander Richard E. Byrd of the
United States Navy, and he put his faith in an aeroplane
fitted with skis instead of wheels.

By 1926 Byrd already had some experience of flying in the
Arctic, for he had been a member of an expedition which
surveyed parts of Greenland from the air. This expedition had
aroused his interest in Arctic flying, with all its problems of
bad weather and navigational difficulties. Richard Byrd had
learned to fly in the Navy but regarded himself as a navigator,
so it was a great challenge to fly over unmapped regions in a
part of the world where a compass was unreliable. Incidentally, when a compass points to the north, it is pointing to the
magnetic North Pole which is some distance from the actual
Pole. To make matters worse, compass needles are very
unsteady near the magnetic Pole. Byrd's pilot was called
Floyd Bennett, and their aircraft was a three-engined Fokker
F.VII/3m airliner which had been bought for Byrd by Edsel
Ford (son of Henry Ford the motor car manufacturer) and
christened 'Josephine Ford'. By May 1926 both Amundsen
and Byrd had established bases at Kings Bay, Spitsbergen –
an island about half-way between Norway and the North
Pole. Byrd was having trouble with the skis on his aircraft and
Amundsen very generously lent him one of his own men,
Bernt Balchen, who was an expert on aircraft skis. Balchen
became very friendly with Byrd and they flew together for
many years.

Both expeditions worked hard on their preparations, each
hoping to be the first to reach the Pole. Byrd was ready first,
and at 1 a.m. on 9th May, 1926, his large monoplane roared
down the snow-covered runway and headed for the north. As
a result of his previous Arctic flying, Byrd decided to use a
special bubble sextant and a sun compass to help in steering an
accurate course over the vast stretches of ice and snow. Just as
they were nearing the Pole one of their oil tanks started to leak
and this set Byrd a difficult question. Should he risk a landing

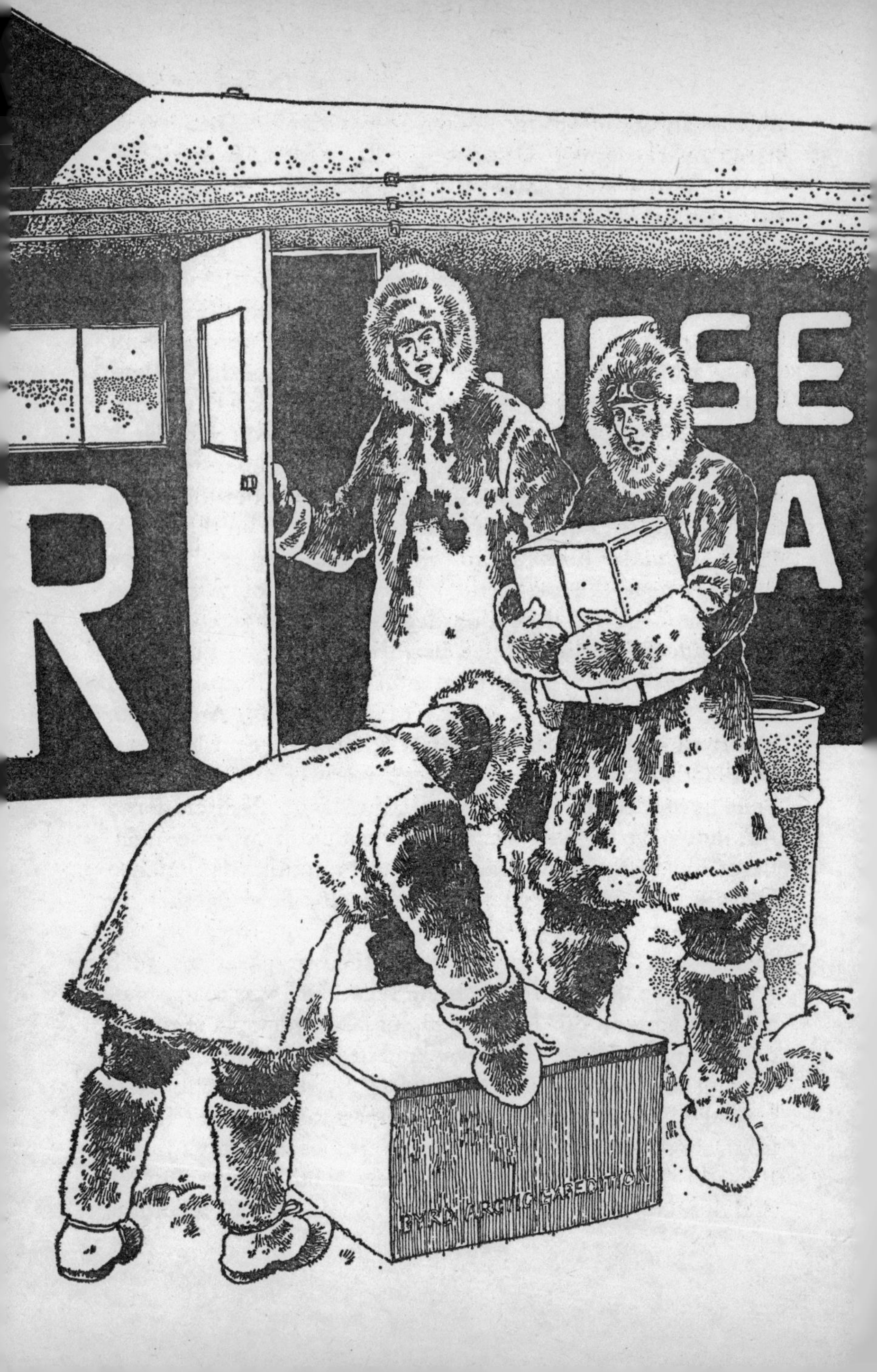
BYRD ARCTIC EXPEDITION

on the rough surface of the ice and mend the leak, or would it be safer to fly on and hope that the oil would last out? He chose to fly on. By 9 a.m. according to Byrd's calculations they were over the North Pole, so they circled around the area and dropped a flag. Later investigations have questioned whether Byrd was in fact precisely over the North Pole as he claimed. Of course there is no 'pole', nor is there any other landmark to pin-point one's position – just a vast expanse of ice and snow. However, Byrd had other problems at the time because his bubble sextant had fallen off his chart-table during one of the turns and was of no further use. Luckily he was an outstanding navigator and he guided Bennett back towards their base. Spitsbergen appeared ahead of them on schedule and they landed safely at 4.30 p.m., having covered 2500 kilometres. Amundsen and his companions rushed out to congratulate the Americans. Although Amundsen had been beaten to the Pole he continued with his plans. The airship *Norge* took off two days later, reached the North Pole and then flew on to Alaska.

Byrd returned to the United States where he was given a great welcome, awarded the Congressional Medal of Honor, and later promoted to Rear Admiral. Being a public hero made it easier to raise money and Byrd did not waste any time in starting to organise an expedition to fly over the South Pole. But before tackling this flight, he decided to fly across the Atlantic. His friend and pilot Floyd Bennett had died of pneumonia, so Bernt Balchen (Amundsen's pilot) joined Byrd and flew with him on the Atlantic flight. In June 1927 they reached France after flying for forty-two hours.

The Antarctic expedition was a large operation made up of sixty men, two ships and no less than four aircraft. Of these, one was another three-engined airliner rather like the Fokker F.VII used for the Arctic flights, but this new aircraft was an American Ford 4-AT Trimotor christened *Floyd Bennett*. The other three aircraft were smaller single-engined machines intended for local surveying flights. The expedition set out in

October 1928, and their first task was to set up a base which they called Little America. From this base, survey flights were made to map some of the unknown territory in the Continent of Antarctica. In March 1929 one of the smaller aircraft flown by Balchen made a forced landing in a blizzard, and for eight days the crew of three were lost. Just when hopes were fading Byrd found them and flew them back to safety. Then the winter set in.

By November the weather improved and survey flying started again. The big Ford Trimotor was prepared for the long flight to the South Pole, and emergency food supplies for several months were loaded on board. At 4 p.m. on 28th November, 1929, the heavily-loaded aircraft took off with Balchen as pilot, Byrd navigating and two other crew members. They dropped some supplies to one of their ground bases and headed for the Pole. Unfortunately they had to cross a range of mountains and could not climb high enough. Byrd had once again to make a difficult decision. Should they turn back or lighten the aircraft by throwing overboard their emergency food supplies? Byrd decided to throw the food overboard and hope that they were not forced down. Luckily his gamble paid off, and after ten hours the Trimotor was circling the South Pole. On this flight the aircraft was fitted with a radio, so the good news was transmitted back to the base at little America and from there to the rest of the world. The Trimotor returned safely and Richard Byrd thus became the first man to reach both Poles by air. He returned to the Antarctic several times on surveying expeditions before he died, an international hero, in 1957.

21 Flight over Everest

In 1933 a British expedition set out to conquer Mount Everest, which is the highest mountain in the world, with a summit 29,028 feet (8848 metres) above sea-level. Unlike most expeditions this one was not aiming to climb the mountain – instead the members were planning to fly over the peak and take a series of photographs which would help to produce a map of the area.

Many difficulties had to be faced even before take-off. To start with an aircraft was needed which could climb to 30,000 feet (9000 metres), and it had to be reliable, for the Himalayas were no place to make a forced landing. It was decided to take two aircraft, both built by Westland Aircraft Ltd of Yeovil in Somerset, who had considerable experience of building rugged biplanes suitable for army cooperation work. One of their Wapitis was the first aircraft to fly through the notorious Khyber Pass on India's North-West Frontier during 1929. The two aircraft chosen were both large biplanes, each fitted with a Bristol Pegasus engine, supercharged to provide extra power in the rarefied air found at high altitudes. One of these aircraft was a Wallace, which was an improved version of the well-tried Wapiti, while the other was a P.V.3 torpedo-carrier. (P.V. stood for Private Venture.) Both were specially prepared for the expedition: military equipment was removed, an oxygen supply was installed for the crews to breathe and the rear cockpits were closed in – the pilots still sat in open cockpits!

Mount Everest was not in British territory: it was divided between Nepal and Tibet, and neither of these countries encouraged visitors. However, in August 1932 the rulers of Nepal agreed to let the expedition fly over their land. This was one major obstacle overcome, but the expedition still had another problem – shortage of money. The situation was saved by Lady Houston, who acted as a 'fairy godmother' to a number of aviation projects including the British Schneider Trophy team in 1931. Once again the generosity of Lady Houston saved the day, and in her honour the P.V.3 became known as the Houston-Westland.

Before the Houston-Everest expedition left Britain all the equipment was thoroughly tested including the heated flying suits for the crews, the oxygen equipment and the cameras. The aircraft too were tested for their ordeal, and on one occasion the Houston-Westland was taken up to a height of 35,000 feet (about 10,600 metres). Once everything was ready the two aircraft, together with all the supplies and equipment, were taken by ship to Karachi. Here the aircraft were re-assembled and flown to a base camp near Purnea in Bihar – some 240 kilometres south of the Himalayas. The leader of the expedition, Air Commodore P. F. M. Fellowes, organised the final preparations and in particular a survey of the weather conditions, for the pilots would have to contend with sudden storms, swirling mists and gale-force winds. There were also some very strong down-currents of air to be avoided, because these could send an aircraft crashing into the mountainside. After much hard work the preparations were completed and all the crews needed was good weather, but they had a long wait.

Eventually the weather cleared, and soon after 8 a.m. on 3rd April, 1933, the two Westland biplanes took off. The Houston-Westland (P.V.3) was piloted by Squadron Leader The Marquess of Douglas and Clydesdale M.P., with Lieutenant-Colonel L. V. S. Blacker as his observer. The Wallace was flown by Flight-Lieutenant J. McIntyre and he was accompanied by Mr S. R. Bonnett, the aerial photographer of the Gaumont-British Film Corporation. The two aircraft climbed steadily upwards through a ground haze and it was not until they reached a height of 19,000 feet (about 5800 metres) that they emerged from the swirling mist into brilliant sunshine. The sight was awe-inspiring, with crystal glaciers, dark crevasses and towering peaks. But they were still some way from their objective, in height if not in distance, and upwards they climbed. They passed near several high peaks including Kangchenjunga, the world's third highest mountain at 28,168 feet (8586 metres). Then as they were flying over Lhotse, which is one of the mountains in the same group as Everest, the two aircraft ran into one of the powerful downcurrents. The pilots increased their engine power and with full-throttle were only just managing to maintain height, but very gradually they started to climb again. Soon after 10 a.m. they reached the summit of Mount Everest and flew just thirty metres above it, but their work was not finished, for their aim was to take photographs. The two aircraft circled the mountain for some time and Bonnett took his pictures despite losing his oxygen supply while flying over the summit.

Having conquered Everest by air the two Westland biplanes returned to their base at Purnea, where they landed at about 11.30 a.m. In just over three hours four men had been to the summit of Everest and back – a far cry from the attempts to reach the summit by land. Many mountaineering expeditions spent weeks climbing on the dangerous faces of Everest only to be driven down again by the difficult conditions. It was not until 1953 that Everest was conquered by land, when Edmund Hillary and Sherpa Tenzing Norkhay reached the summit.

The 1933 Houston-Everest Flight did not return home immediately, because the crew planned to take more aerial photographs. The next day both aircraft were airborne again but with different crews, except for Bonnett, the photographer. This time the target was Kangchenjunga. Then on 19th

April it was decided to make another flight over Everest, although official permission had not been given. The crews were the same as for the first flight except for A. L. Fisher, another photographer, who replaced Bonnett. Lord Clydesdale wanted to obtain a series of overlapping vertical photographs which would provide a complete survey of the area towards the summit. Fisher was taking these vertical pictures almost all the time while Colonel Blacker took some vertical pictures as well as more conventional views. With many impressive photographs to show for their hard work, the Houston-Everest flight returned to Britain.

The two Westland biplanes which had served the expedition so well were not pensioned off. The Wallace was converted back into a standard aircraft with a rear cockpit for an air-gunner and then went into service with the RAF. A more unusual fate befell the P.V.3, for it became a flying 'test-bed', into which experimental Bristol engines were fitted in order to test them in the air.

22 Walking in Space

'A delicate blue halo surrounds the Earth, merging with the blackness of space in which the stars are bright and clear cut.' These were the words of Yuri Gagarin, the first man to travel in space. Yuri Gagarin saw the earth as no one had seen it before, from inside his 'Vostok' spacecraft while it completed a single orbit at a height ranging from 170 to 315 kilometres. Following Gagarin's historic flight of 1961 several men and one woman travelled in space, but four years passed before anyone ventured out of a spacecraft and into 'the blackness of space'.

In the early 1960s both Russians and Americans were carrying out a series of manned space flights using small spacecraft capable of putting one person into space. The Russians were ahead in the so-called space race with their Vostok spacecraft, similar to the one used by Gagarin. By 1963 they had achieved several long space flights including one of eighty-one orbits, while the best flight by an American Mercury spacecraft was twenty-two orbits. Both countries then turned their attention to larger spacecraft, and the Russians continued to lead the way with their new 'Voskhod'. On 12th October, 1964, Voskhod 1 lifted off from the Baikonur cosmodrome carrying into space a crew of three – a cosmonaut, a scientist and a doctor. (The Russians call their spacemen cosmonauts while the Americans use the name astronauts.) The flight lasted just over twenty-four hours, during which time the spacecraft completed sixteen orbits of the Earth.

On 18th March, 1965, there was a heavy blizzard at the Baikonur cosmodrome, but by 10 a.m. the weather cleared and Voskhod 2 was launched. On board were the two cosmonauts Pavel Belyayev and Aleksei Leonov, each wearing a new type of spacesuit and space helmet. Voskhod 2 differed from Voskhod 1 because it had been fitted with an airlock, through which Leonov planned to leave the spacecraft and walk in space. No one knew how a man's mind and body would stand up to the emptiness of space – some scientists forecast that it would cause insanity. Leonov had been given a long series of tests to ensure that he was ready for the unknown. On several occasions he had spent days and even weeks all alone in a soundproof room, totally isolated from the outside world but observed by psychologists. After one of these sessions Leonov was rushed to an airfield, flown to a high altitude and ejected from the aircraft. As he floated down on his parachute he remained calm and cheerful – nothing seemed to upset him.

As Voskhod 2 was making its second orbit of the Earth, Leonov strapped on his back-pack which contained all the equipment needed to keep him alive in space including a supply of oxygen. Belyayev gave him a helping hand and then they opened the inner door of the airlock. 'Well, go ahead, Aleksei!' said Belyayev, and Leonov floated headfirst into the opening. Of course he was weightless so his movements were very different from normal, but the cosmonauts had practised moving under similar conditions during their training programme. Once Leonov's feet had disappeared, Belyayev closed the inside door, dropped the pressure and released the outside hatch.

Leonov was immediately impressed by the brightness of the sun, even though he was wearing a darkened visor on his space helmet. As his head emerged through the opening he could see that the sky was black except for the brilliant stars.

His progress was being televised and transmitted back down to the ground and he was enjoying his experience. 'I can see the Caucasus (mountains),' he said as he looked down on the Earth, and then he reported that he could see the Black Sea very clearly.

But this was not a sightseeing trip – there was work to be done. Leonov's next task was to fix a film camera to the outside of the spacecraft so that his 'extra-vehicular activity' (E.V.A.) could be filmed. Once this was done he emerged completely from the hatch and floated away from the Voskhod – only a few centimetres at first. Then, as his confidence grew, he drifted away to the full extent of the five-metre safety line which connected him to his spacecraft.

So Aleksei Leonov became the first man to walk in space, but 'walk' is hardly the word to describe his antics as he swam, floated, spun like a top and even turned somersaults. His space gymnastics were amusing, but their purpose was to find out whether it was possible for a man to work in space and perhaps repair a damaged spacecraft. Leonov had no problems moving about, but he did find it difficult to concentrate on his work when there were so many exciting things to see. His hobby was painting and he was fascinated by the colours and contrasts of space – everything seemed different. All too soon his walk in space came to an end, for his time limit was ten minutes. However, before getting back into the craft, his last job was to remove the camera and carry it through the airlock. This simple operation nearly led to disaster when the camera got stuck in the entrance of the airlock. For a moment he thought he might have to throw away the camera and its valuable film, but he struggled on until he manoeuvred both the camera and himself back inside. Belyayev promptly reported to Ground Control: 'The mission involving the cosmonaut's extra-vehicular activity and his return to the spacecraft has been fully carried out.' So far, so good, but now it was Belyayev's turn to face a difficult situation.

The Voskhod was scheduled to return to Earth on the

sixteenth orbit under fully automatic control – guided down by instruments and electronic equipment. But just before the retro-rockets were fired to start the spacecraft's re-entry into the Earth's atmosphere it was discovered that one of the vital instruments was not working. This instrument should have set the spacecraft at the correct angle ready for the retro-rockets to fire. The cosmonauts had to make another orbit while Belyayev prepared to bring the spacecraft down under manual control. This was a tricky operation, because he had to manoeuvre the Voskhod into exactly the right position and then fire the retro-rockets. If the angle was too steep the spacecraft would burn up in the earth's atmosphere, but if it was too shallow they would bounce off the air and fly out into space forever. Belyayev, assisted by the cheerful Leonov, made a successful re-entry and the Voskhod descended by parachute into a snow-covered forest. Their flight had lasted twenty-six hours but their troubles were not quite over, for their extra orbit had resulted in a touch-down some distance from the planned position. After about two hours the rescue helicopters found them, and the two cosmonauts returned to Moscow where they were decorated with the highest awards and given a State reception.

23 The Berlin Air Lift 1948-9

During the 1920s airline passenger services started in many countries, but some far-sighted pilots realised that freight could also be carried by air. Of course this was a more expensive method than transporting it by road, rail or canal, but in some parts of the world there were no such means of transport. One such area was Northern Canada, where there were thousands of square kilometres of wild 'bush' country dotted with small hunting communities and mining towns. The pioneering bush pilots carried passengers, mail, food and any equipment light enough for their aircraft to lift. Heavy equipment and bulky products had to be transported by river during the summer months when the ice melted. Over the years more and more aircraft were flying vital supplies to remote communities in many parts of the world and few people ever visualised a major city being supplied entirely by air, yet this happened in 1948 to Berlin.

The story begins at the end of the Second World War when Germany was divided into four zones each controlled by one of the Allied powers – Great Britain, France, the U.S.A. and Russia. The city of Berlin was also divided into four sectors, but it was situated within the Russian zone, like an island, so the British, French and Americans had to pass through Russian-held territory to reach their sectors of Berlin. This was quite satisfactory until the Russians and their former

Allies grew less and less friendly and the 'Cold War' developed. Squabbles at the frontiers were frequent, and from 24th June, 1948, the Russians refused to allow any British, French or American traffic through Eastern Germany to Berlin. With all the roads, railways and canals closed, the only way to reach Berlin was by air. Fortunately the Russians had signed an agreement which gave the Western Allies three air 'corridors' through Eastern Germany, each 32 kilometres wide. The Western Allies had to decide whether to leave Berlin and let the Russians take over, or to supply the city and its two and a quarter million people by air. It was a mammoth undertaking just to fly in food, mail, clothes and medical supplies, but in addition to these domestic items Berlin needed coal, oil, petrol, industrial machines and raw materials. Just to keep the power stations working required 6000 tonnes of coal each week.

Within a few days of the Russian blockade starting, RAF Dakotas and United States Air Force C-47s began delivering essential supplies to the beleaguered city. Incidentally, both these aircraft were variants of the faithful old Douglas DC-3 airliner and they could carry about three and a half tonnes of freight per trip. Early in July, Short Sunderland flying boats from RAF Coastal Command started flying to Berlin where they landed on a lake to unload their five-tonne load. Short Hythe flying boats from Aquila Airways later joined the Sunderlands and this flying boat service continued until the winter, when there was a danger of the lake freezing. The first civilian aircraft joined the air lift late in July, when a number of Avro Lancastrians began to carry petrol to Berlin. The Lancastrian was a civil version of the famous Lancaster bomber which a few years earlier had been bombing the very city its descendant was saving.

As the air lift built up, Berlin's two airfields, Gatow and Tempelhof, were becoming very congested, and it was decided to build a third one on an artillery range in the French sector. The people of Berlin were keen to help, for they had no wish to be ruled by the Russians. About 18,000 citizens started work on the new runway at Tegel on 5th September, and the first aircraft landed just two months later. With three airfields operating and even more aircraft becoming available, a Combined Air Lift Task Force was set up to put the British and American operations under a central control. This was essential because never before had so many aircraft been flying into such a small area. By October there were about 250 aircraft flying to Berlin, representing some ten different types. Most of the American crews were by now flying four-engined Douglas C-54s (military DC-4s), but the British fleet consisted of a very mixed bag. The Air Traffic Control officers had quite a problem, because these assorted aircraft approached the runways at different speeds and yet they had to be landed at the rate of one every two or three minutes round the clock. There was no room for the smallest miscalculation.

During the winter months fog and gale force winds reduced the number of flights considerably, but during the spring of 1949 they increased again and even exceeded the figures achieved in the previous autumn. By this time there were 340 aircraft in use and, of these, 200 were from the USAF, 95 were RAF machines and the remaining 45 were from various airlines. On an average day about 5600 tonnes of cargo were flown into Berlin and, of this, more than a half was coal, while about a quarter consisted of food. Usually each aircraft and crew kept to one kind of cargo, so after several months it was easy to distinguish between a coal-crew and a flour-crew! Salt was originally carried by the flying boats because they were made to withstand the corrosion caused by salt in sea water. When they were withdrawn the salt was transferred to Handley Page Haltons fitted with external panniers which kept the salt well away from the aircraft's structure. In order to save weight, dried foods were used whenever possible and dried potato with sauce became a familiar meal for many Berlin families.

Although food was in short supply and rationed, the people

of Berlin were still better off than they had been during the later war years. The coffee they were receiving by air was far superior to the acorn-coffee they had to drink during the war! They were determined to beat the Russian blockade despite the hardships they had to bear. Sometimes the electricity was turned on for only two hours per day and factories had to close because they were short of coal.

The air lift produced many stories of hardship and friendship, and one of these concerned an American pilot of a C-54. He was talking to some children on the edge of the airfield and was surprised that they did not ask him for any sweets. 'Got any gum, chum?' was a familiar cry to U.S. servicemen. He realised that these children had probably never tasted real sweets, so he gave them some, and they were so delighted that he decided he must try to get some more for them. He told the children to look out for his aircraft the next day and he would drop some sweets for them by a parachute made out of his handkerchief. 'How will we know which is your aircraft?' asked the children. 'I'll wiggle my wings when I come over,' replied the pilot. He kept his promise – the children received their sweets and 'Uncle Wiggly Wings' became a great hero of the Berlin children.

After almost a year the Russians relented and reopened the roads and railways. The air lift had beaten the blockade. Of course it had been expensive and in normal circumstances it would not be practicable to carry coal by air. Nevertheless the Berlin air lift had shown the effectiveness of air transport in a very dramatic way.

24 One thousand miles an hour

Between the years 1906 and 1939 the world air speed record increased from a mere 25 mph (40 kph) to 469 mph (755 kph). It was a very gradual increase, usually in stages of 15 to 30 kph. Then came the Second World War and the invention of the jet engine which increased speeds quite considerably.

The first jet to hold the record was a Gloster Meteor, and with a speed of 606 mph (975 kph) it beat the old record by a margin of 220 kph. Incidentally, this old record had been set up in 1939 by a racing version of the famous German fighter, the Messerschmitt Bf-109. The Meteor's record did not stand for very long, because jet fighters from Britain and the United States vied with each other for the coveted title. By 1955 the record stood at 822 mph (1323 kph) and was held by a North American F-100C Super Sabre jet fighter. Then came a dramatic record-breaking flight by a British research aircraft, the Fairey Delta 2, which beat the old record by 499 kph. For the first time the world air speed record passed the 1000 mph mark and stood at 1132 mph (1822 kph).

The Fairey Aviation Company was well known for its naval aircraft, including the famous Swordfish biplane of the Second World War, but after the war they extended their activities to helicopters and high-speed delta-winged aircraft. A delta wing is triangular in shape and takes its name from the Greek letter 'delta', because the symbol for 'capital delta'

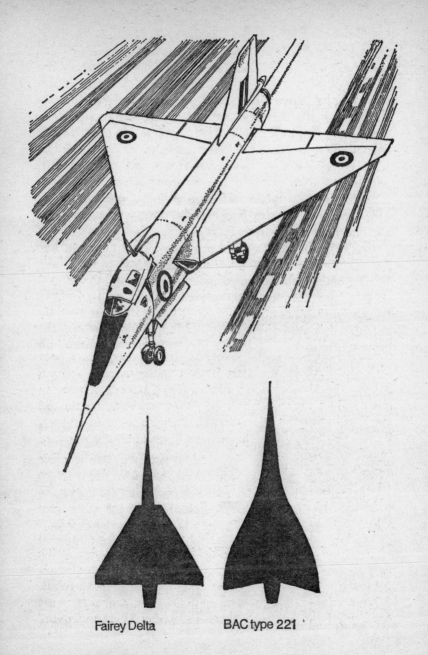

Fairey Delta

BAC type 221

is a triangle. The reason for using this shape is a little more complicated, and concerns the shock-wave which forms when an aircraft flies at the speed of sound. The effects of this shock-wave can be reduced by using a wing which is swept backwards. Now, if a wing is swept back a long way its tip comes very close to the tailplane, so designers came up with the idea of combining wing and tail into one triangular shape – a delta wing. Fairey's tried out this idea in 1951 with their tiny F.D.1, which had a delta wing but retained a small tailplane mounted high on the fin. Their next 'delta' was completely different, for it was very long and did not have a tailplane at all. The first Fairey F.D.2 (Fairey Delta 2) was flown by Peter Twiss on 6th October, 1954, and was followed by a second one sixteen months later. Another unusual feature of the Fairey Delta 2 design was its hinged cockpit, which could be angled down to give the pilot a better view on landing. In order to fly slowly, the pilot of a delta-winged aircraft has to keep his machine in a nose-up attitude, and it is difficult to see the ground. The hinged nose was a very successful solution to this problem, and a modified version was later used on Concorde.

During 1955 it became obvious to the Fairey design team that their aircraft could easily beat the current speed record of 822 mph (1323 kph) and become the first 1000 mph record holder. They decided to go ahead, but kept their plans secret just in case the Americans might try to forestall them. All the timing and photographic equipment was prepared under a 'cover story' produced to hide the real purpose. Many of the engineers actually working on the aircraft itself did not realise until two days before the attempt why so much hard work had been carried out. The Fairey Delta 2 was based at Boscombe Down, a Government experimental establishment near Amesbury, and the course for the record attempt lay along the south coast. Timing cameras were installed at each end of the course, one near Chichester and the other almost ten miles away at Ford. On 10th March, 1956, everything was ready and Peter Twiss made his first run from Chichester to Ford at 38,000 feet (11,582 metres). It took him about thirty seconds and his speed was recorded at 1117.6 mph (1798.6 kph). He then made a sweeping turn out to sea and returned along the coast. This time his speed was 1146.9 mph (1845.7 kph), an average of 1132 mph (1822.8 kph) or Mach 1.731. The record had been shattered.

By this time the second Fairey Delta 2 was flying and the two aircraft continued with a research programme into super-sonic flight. By 1960 they had completed most of their work and at the same time a new wing shape needed to be tested. This was called a 'slender delta' wing and was intended for a new generation of supersonic airliners, including the Con-corde. Before building a supersonic airliner the British authorities decided to carry out flight tests using two small aircraft each fitted with the new slender delta wing. For the slow-speed tests they ordered a Handley Page H.P.115, a comparatively cheap aircraft designed for the job. Because there was a shortage of money it was decided not to build a new high-speed aircraft, but to modify the Fairey Delta 2.

In September 1960 the record-breaking Fairey Delta 2 was flown to the Filton Airfield of the British Aircraft Corporation and work began on the conversion. A new wing was designed and fitted with the graceful shape now a familiar sight on Concorde. Other changes had to be made such as a length-ened fuselage and longer undercarriage legs. The much-modified Fairey Delta 2 became the BAC.221, and on 1st May, 1964, it made its first flight. A long programme of test flying began in order to study the flow of air over a slender delta wing. Tiny holes were drilled in the wing surface to measure the air pressures and check the predictions made by the aerodynamicists. The flow of air was studied by sticking woollen tufts to the wing surface and filming it during flight trials. Any areas of turbulence could easily be spotted.

Both Fairey Delta 2s finished their days in museums. The unmodified aircraft is with the RAF and the BAC.221 the Royal Scottish Museum of Flight, East Fortune Airfield.

25 Supersonic passengers – the Concorde story

When a name was needed for the new supersonic airliner designed by a joint British and French team, 'Concorde' was chosen because it meant agreement or harmony, yet no aircraft in history has ever been involved in so many arguments and controversies! Even the name caused a problem when it was first selected, because the British used 'Concord' while the French version was 'Concorde'. In the interests of harmony 'Concorde' was accepted by both countries. The project started quite separately in Britain and France way back in 1956, then in 1962 the two governments signed an agreement to share the design and construction work. Without this agreement Concorde would probably never have been built, because sharing the work also included sharing the costs, which would have been too high for one country to bear.

Why build a supersonic airliner anyway? The simple answer is that people are always looking for ways of saving time, and the faster we travel, the more time we save. Supersonic airliners reduce many journey times by half and this is equivalent to shrinking the earth to half its size. For example, a journey from London to New York takes about eight hours by jet airliner and this uses most of one day, whereas a supersonic airliner takes only four hours. A business man could fly to New York, attend a meeting and return to London all in the same day. Times become very confusing when travelling

at supersonic speeds, because the airliner moves across the surface of the earth faster than the sun. New York time is five hours behind London time, so if a supersonic airliner leaves London at 8 a.m. and takes four hours for the journey, it arrives in New York at 12 noon (London time), which is 7 a.m. in New York. Strange though it sounds, the passenger arrives one hour before leaving – just in time for a second breakfast! Of course flying in the opposite direction adds time to the journey.

Flying at supersonic speeds does have certain technical problems, such as the high air resistance (or drag) encountered as the aircraft reaches the speed of sound (Mach 1.0), and of course the sonic boom heard on the ground. But keeping passengers and aircraft cool is also a major problem. At very high speeds the friction between the air and the airliner's skin generates enough heat to raise the temperature of the skin above the boiling point of water. To keep the inside of the passenger cabin at a comfortable temperature, the skin has to be lagged and a refrigeration system installed. However, the effect of this heat on the metal airframe is more serious, because the strength of the aluminium alloys used in aircraft construction drops very rapidly as the temperature rises. At temperatures over 100°C these aluminium alloys become too weak to use, and this temperature corresponds to a speed of about Mach 2 (twice the speed of sound). If a Mach 3 airliner were designed its skin temperature would reach 200°C and this would force the designers to build it from stainless steel or the relatively new metal titanium. The British and French designers of Concorde decided to keep to the traditional aluminium alloys and a speed of Mach 2, which is 1300 mph (2092 kph) or London to Edinburgh in eighteen minutes.

To drive an airliner carrying a hundred passengers through the air at this incredible speed requires engines of great power, and in the case of Concorde this power is supplied by four Rolls-Royce (Bristol)/Snecma Olympus engines. One of these engines supplies a thrust of 38,000 lb (about 17,235 kilos) during take-off, which is just about the same power as the four engines used to power the De Havilland Comet airliner. When a new engine is designed it must be tested in flight, but until its reliability has been fully proved it is seldom used as the only source of power. In the case of the Olympus for Concorde, an engine complete with complex intake and exhaust systems was fitted beneath the fuselage of an Avro Vulcan bomber. This flying test-bed ensured that the Olympus was thoroughly tested before it was used in Concorde itself.

By the time Concorde started carrying passengers in January 1976 it had been more thoroughly tested and proven than any previous commercial aircraft. Ten years were spent on rigorous ground testing and almost four thousand hours in the air during the extensive test flying programme which made use of no less than seven aircraft. Nevertheless there are still problems – the sonic boom, the noise of four huge engines during take-off, high operating costs and possible pollution of the upper atmosphere. The Concorde has always been a controversial aircraft, but passengers who have sampled supersonic travel are full of praise for the smooth ride – even when they break through the so-called sound barrier.

More Beaver Books

We hope you have enjoyed this Beaver Book. Here are some of the other titles:

Air Quiz   A Beaver original. Questions on flying, from the early days of balloons to supersonic planes and space rockets, by J. E. Thompson. Illustrated throughout by John Batchelor

My Favourite Escape Stories   Pat Reid, author of *The Colditz Story*, presents his favourite true stories from four hundred years of escapes. Gripping reading for everyone from nine upwards.

Making and Flying Kites   How to make and fly sixteen different kites, from the traditional Hargrave box kite to the exciting Nagasaki fighting kite, by A. Lloyd, C. Mitchell and N. Thomas

Wild Lone   'BB's' classic depiction of the life of a fox in hunting countryside, for older readers. The author's book *The Lord of the Forest* is also available in Beavers

Storm Warning   A powerful novel for older readers set in pre-war Nazi Germany, about a young English girl who helps two Jewish children escape from the Gestapo. By Mara Kay

A Witch in the Family   The Stanley children find their new step-sister rather odd. For Amanda's great interest is the supernatural, and her arrival brings some unexpected changes. A winner of the Newbery Honor Medal, this is a funny yet sensitive story for readers of ten upwards by Zilpha Keatley Snyder

New Beavers are published every month, and if you would like the *Beaver Bulletin* – which gives all the details – please send a large stamped addressed envelope to:

Beaver Bulletin
The Hamlyn Group
Astronaut House
Feltham
Middlesex TW14 9AR

336131